"The book will be of great interest to academics who have an interest in audit, particularly public audit. There will also be practitioner interest, particularly in the analysis of international perspectives".

– *Pat Barrett*, former Auditor-General of Australia

"Public sector auditing currently has significant pressures and stresses associated with emerging social, demographic, economic, technological, and environmental challenges. This textbook presents several theoretical and practical contributions to knowledge of public sector auditing. The book provides a contemporary public sector auditing perspective that is geared to include the current and future challenges and provide significant insights for scholars and public sector actors to strategically decide on the many dynamic challenges".

– *Giuseppe Grossi*, Professor, Nord University, Norway, and Kristianstad University, Sweden

"There is a dearth of academic research on public sector auditing. This text will be of great value to SAIs, policy makers, and the academic community in developing the critical role that SAIs play in systems of country governance."

– *Robert Buchanan*, Chairperson, New Zealand Auditing and Assurance Standards Board

Public Sector Audit

This book provides a concise overview of the current context and types of public sector audit and the varied structures within which public sector audit is practised across the world.

It summarises the objectives of public sector audit as well as explores the role of the International Organisation of Supreme Audit Institutions in providing guidance to these. Drawing on public and private sector audit as well as the views of academics and practitioners on public sector audit, it provides a unique research-based guide to the current issues and future challenges in the field.

Carolyn J. Cordery is Professor in Accounting at Aston University, UK. Her main research focuses on not-for-profit organisations' accounting and accountability. She is interested in how these organisations are resourced, the resource constraints that cause many of these organisations to be financially vulnerable and the regulatory environment in which they work. Carolyn also researches in the public sector, particularly in audit arrangements and how they can enhance accountability. She is Joint Editor of *Accounting History* and is Associate Editor of *British Accounting Review*.

David C. Hay is Professor of Auditing at the University of Auckland, New Zealand. He is the Editor-in-Chief of the *International Journal of Auditing*. He has published about 50 articles in refereed research journals. David's research interests include auditing issues internationally and in New Zealand, including auditor independence, corporate governance and public sector auditing. He is also the editor of the *Routledge Companion to Auditing* (2014) and *The Future of Auditing* (2019). David is a member of the New Zealand Auditing and Assurance Standards Board.

Routledge Focus on Accounting and Auditing

Advances in the fields of accounting and auditing as areas of research and education, alongside shifts in the global economy present a constantly shifting environment. This presents challenges for scholars and practitioners trying to keep up with the latest important insights in both theory and professional practice. Routledge Focus on Accounting and Auditing presents concise texts on key topics in the world of accounting research.

Individually, each title in the series provides coverage of a key topic in accounting and auditing, whilst collectively, the series forms a comprehensive collection across the discipline of accounting.

The Boundaries in Financial and Non-Financial Reporting
A Comparative Analysis of their Constitutive Role
Laura Girella

The Future of Auditing
David Hay

Accounting Regulation in Japan
Evolution and Development from 2001 to 2015
Masatsugu Sanada and Yoshihiro Tokuga

Gender and Corporate Governance
Francisco Bravo Urquiza and Nuria Reguera-Alvarado

Accounting, Representation and Responsibility
Deleuze and Guattarí Perspectives
Niels Joseph Lennon

Public Sector Audit
Carolyn J. Cordery and David C. Hay

For more information about this series, please visit: www.routledge.com/Routledge-Focus-on-Accounting-and-Auditing/book-series/RFAA

Public Sector Audit

Carolyn J. Cordery
and David C. Hay

Routledge
Taylor & Francis Group
LONDON AND NEW YORK

First published 2021
by Routledge
2 Park Square, Milton Park, Abingdon, Oxon OX14 4RN

and by Routledge
52 Vanderbilt Avenue, New York, NY 10017

Routledge is an imprint of the Taylor & Francis Group, an informa business

British Library Cataloguing-in-Publication Data
A catalogue record for this book is available from the British Library

Library of Congress Cataloging-in-Publication Data
Names: Cordery, Carolyn, author. | Hay, David, 1955– author.
Title: Public sector audit/Carolyn J. Cordery and David C. Hay.
Description: Abingdon, Oxon ; New York, NY : Routledge, 2021. | Series: Routledge focus on accounting and auditing | Includes bibliographical references and index.
Identifiers: LCCN 2020031110 (print) | LCCN 2020031111 (ebook)
Subjects: LCSH: Finance, Public – Auditing. | Public administration – Evaluation.
Classification: LCC HJ9733 .H37 2021 (print) | LCC HJ9733 (ebook) | DDC 657/.835045 – dc23
LC record available at https://lccn.loc.gov/2020031110
LC ebook record available at https://lccn.loc.gov/2020031111

ISBN: 978-0-367-19291-4 (hbk)
ISBN: 978-0-429-20163-9 (ebk)

Typeset in Times New Roman
by Apex CoVantage, LLC

Contents

Acknowledgements

There are many people to thank for the inspiration and completion of this book. Our good colleague Adjunct Professor and ex-Deputy Auditor General of New Zealand Kevin Simpkins was someone who personified the excellence of public sector audit. Due to Kevin's untimely death in October 2015, we ended up working together on the Centre for Accounting and Governance Research (CAGTR) project for New Zealand's Office of the Auditor General (OAG) on the 'value of public sector audit'. This allowed for a re-kindling of David's interest in public sector audit and was the first major Supreme Audit Institution (SAI) research project that Carolyn undertook. It would be fair to say that both of us found the SAI world to be fascinating. We thank Tony van Zijl, Professor of Accounting and Finance at Victoria University, for this opportunity and Ann Webster (then the Assistant Auditor-General, Research and Development), who was also a member of the CAGTR Board and enthusiastically introduced this project. We also thank Lyn Provost – at the time the Comptroller and Auditor-General – who funded and supported this research. OAG staff were also helpful in informing us during that research, but Deputy Auditor-General Greg Schollum and Karen Smith, Research Officer, have continued to encourage us to research on the functions of the SAIs, and we are grateful to them.

This book draws on data from the International Organisation of SAIs (INTOSAI), and we are grateful that it allowed us to access data on characteristics of SAIs. Director of the INTOSAI General Secretariat Dr Monika González-Koss and Mr Francisco T. Parral-Pineda, Departmental Chief of the National Anti-Corruption System Division of the Auditoria Superior de la Federacíon, very helpfully provided access to INTOSAI's database maintained by the SAI of Mexico. We are extremely grateful to Jika Mapila, Chief Auditor of the Malawi National Audit Office, who assisted us in data collection. We also present data in this book from a survey of INTOSAI members, and we thank them for spending time to share their thoughts which have helped us, especially in understanding the opportunities and challenges for SAIs' future.

Portions of this book have been shared in various presentations. Specifically, the messages in Chapter 4 formed a plenary presented at the International Research Society for Public Management's (IRSPM's) VII Annual SIG Workshop on Accounting and Accountability in October 2019 and in a Business Graduates Association (BGA) trailblazer webinar in April 2020. Key messages from Chapters 2 and 3 formed the plenary presented at the Comparative International Government Accounting Research (CIGAR) Workshop in June 2020. We are grateful for feedback from colleagues in these sessions and in other discussions.

Carolyn J. Cordery and David C. Hay

1 Introduction

1.1 Introduction to the chapter

Almost 200 countries around the world operate Supreme Audit Institutions (SAIs) which are responsible for compliance and performance audits of various public sector agencies and government as a whole, and often a raft of local government and other government-funded entities (The World Bank, 2001). The International Organisation of SAIs (INTOSAI) states that SAIs' overall objectives should be to promote good governance and effective public services to users (INTOSAI, 2004, p. 33). In different countries, the structures and responsibilities of SAIs differ, but they share a general responsibility to strengthen accountability, transparency and integrity in public sector entities. Internationally, they are supported in their functions by the operations of INTOSAI and its regional bodies.[1] It is the purpose of this introductory chapter to provide an overview of the different structures to lay a foundation for the rest of the book which considers in more detail the reasons for public sector audit, the current context in which SAIs operate and how this will affect their future operations. This chapter also outlines the typical types of audit undertaken by SAIs as well as the public sector auditees that may be the subject of the SAI's concern. In this chapter we review what is known from the previous literature, while in the remaining chapters we add to the existing published research.

1.2 Structures

The most commonly discussed SAI structure is the Westminster model, which emanates from the United Kingdom (UK). It comprises an independent statutory body with "a Comptroller and Auditor General who is an officer of the House of Commons" (Pollitt and Summa, 1997, p. 315). The reports of these SAIs are discussed at the Public Accounts Committee (or similar) of Parliament. Pollitt and Summa (1997) note a variant on this model in the Swedish and Finnish SAIs which were at that time part of government, as they were within their respective Ministries of Finance but operated with independence. They report to parliamentary auditors. The Westminster model is used in many Commonwealth countries, as well as, *inter alia*, Mexico, Chile and Poland (Effective Institutions Platform, 2014).

The board model has similarities to the Westminster system, but a panel (or board) replaces the single auditor-general. This is evident, for example, in Argentina, Japan and the Netherlands (Effective Institutions Platform, 2014). In the board model, the SAI typically reports to the cabinet which then submits the reports to the legislature. Arthur *et al.* (2012) note that this is not always the case, as Norway, which follows the board model, submits reports directly to Parliament. This model is also replicated in the European Court of Audit (ECA) which is a supra-national institution responsible for auditing European Union institutions.

The court or Napoleonic system is used in Latin countries within Europe, many French-speaking countries and Latin America. It comprises a Court of Audit with judges and legal staff. Their court status provides high levels of influence, especially as the magistrates may be appointed for life, can have long civil careers and are highly educated (Morin, 2011). Countries with the court model include France, Brazil, Greece and Turkey (Effective Institutions Platform, 2014).

Despite the differences in structure, there is a push for SAIs to be independent from government both in terms of appointment and remuneration (Clark *et al.*, 2007). The belief is that this will underpin audit quality; nevertheless, Clark *et al.* (2007) found diversity across European SAIs and recommended changes to relevant legislation to boost SAI authority and independence. It is likely that this variety in one set of SAIs will be replicated internationally.

1.3 Types of audit undertaken

The types of audit undertaken are linked to the mission of the SAI. Some report only to Parliament, while others expect to serve a wider set of stakeholders, including the taxpayer and the public. The three basic audit types are compliance audits (pre-audit and post-audit), financial statement audits and performance audits.

Historically, SAI audit activity included pre-audit activities (*a priori*) to check compliance with expenditure policies and thus to ensure probity pre-expenditure rather than post-expenditure. These compliance pre-audit activities remain important in some economies, for example, Belgium and Greece (Groenendijk, 2004) (as discussed further in Chapter 3). Other compliance audits undertaken by SAIs include those typically seen in the private sector, to ensure compliance with debt covenants or for specific stakeholders.

Financial auditing is undertaken to ensure the probity of funds spent by government institutions (that is, that they are spent correctly within the budget allocation) and provide assertions that the financial statements of their auditees faithfully represent (or show a true and fair view) in the agency-related relationship between government employees as agents for the tax-paying public principals. Typically, SAIs expect public sector entities to operate their own internal audit, rather than being involved in this themselves (Sterck and Bouckaert, 2006). Naturally, assessment of the quality of the internal audit is part of a systems-based external audit.

The advent of New Public Management (NPM) from the mid-1970s (first in the UK and United States (US), but later in other countries) brought with it a focus on public sector performance, including efficiency and effectiveness as well as economy (Pollitt and Summa, 1997). As such, performance audits are now an increasingly significant element in many SAIs' work plans (Barrett, 1996). The remit of performance audits varies widely and encompasses operational, management and 'value for money' (VFM) audits. Further, how these audits are undertaken differs between SAIs. For some, performance audits are part of their compliance financial statement audit (especially when this already includes an audit of non-financial indicators); for others, a separate internal unit undertakes performance audits on matters that are relevant to develop efficiency and effectiveness within government; and for a third set of SAIs, performance audits may be undertaken by a mix of the separate internal unit and also the general audit teams. While SAIs decline to critique policy, as this could impair their independence (Cordery and Hay, 2018), these performance audits cover a wide range of evaluation and audit functions (Barzelay, 1997).

One area where VFM/performance audits have increased is in that of Public Private Partnerships (PPP) or Private Finance Initiatives (PFI), an area of funding for public infrastructure that has increased in the 1990s and reflects NPM principles (Shaoul *et al.*, 2008). SAIs are called upon to assess compliance with the terms of such contracts, although Shaoul *et al.* (2008) note that the penalties for non-compliance tend to be limited. SAIs are also called upon to assess the VFM or performance of these contracts when they have been in existence for a period. Issues raised for auditing include whether or not the financing is on the balance sheet (and whose), who bears the risks and at what stage (Shaoul *et al.*, 2008), whether the contract is delivered on time (if for construction) and whether service levels are in line with expectations (in order to agree on the profit-sharing calculations and to inform future contracts) (Grimsey and Lewis, 2005). English (2007) notes that SAIs frequently do not have the mandate to audit beyond the implementation of a PPP's objectives to auditing its effectiveness. Hence, performance audit has frequently been used to investigate the pre-contract stage rather than post-contracting (English, 2007), although as these long-term projects come to their end, this balance may change.

While performance audits are a means for reforms to become embedded in public sector practices, Funnell (2015) notes the influence of governments on the topics chosen for performance audits and the way in which they are carried out. As a political endeavour, this can also depend on how the SAI is appointed and resourced and its ability to critique government (Mulgan, 2001). Assuming that this is so, Schelker and Eichenberger (2010) make a strong case for public sector auditors not only to provide an ex-ante audit of state budgets but also to evaluate individual policy proposals, as is the current practice in Switzerland.

Lastly, although change may be a natural outcome of performance audit, the dual goals of accountability (under agency theory) and improving performance may be at odds (Raudla *et al.*, 2016). Nevertheless, auditees are reported to generally find them useful (Reichborn-Kjennerud, 2013; Morin, 2016; Raudla *et al.*, 2016).

1.4 Types of auditees and approach

While the terminology of 'Supreme Audit Institution' suggests a sole national audit body responsible for government accounts, the meaning of the term 'government' differs considerably. For example, the National Audit Office (NAO) in the UK audits all central government departments, agencies and other public bodies and as well establishes the Code of Practice for local government auditors and undertakes performance audits of local boards and authorities. Between 1983 and 2015, the Audit Commission handled local government issues.[2] In much the same way, state auditors undertake audits of state bodies in, for example, the US and Australia, while these countries' SAIs audit federal or Commonwealth activities. State structures are also evident in the court model, as can be seen in Brazil, which has 31 state audit courts with many auditees under their jurisdictions and, in most cases, reasonably large staff numbers (Melo *et al.*, 2009).

To the extent there are state auditors, it is apparent they may have different roles from the federal auditors (SAIs) (Friedberg and Lutrin, 2005) and receive their mandate in different ways (as already noted) (Funnell, 2015). They may or may not be involved in performance audits (Mulgan, 2001). In addition, sub-national auditing may be outsourced to private sector auditors (as is the case in the UK since 2015). For example, Paananen (2016) presents information on modified audit reports in Finnish local government (hospital) audits undertaken by private sector auditors. Further, SAIs also frequently employ private sector auditors as an audit resource.

There is also a wide range of different entities which can be covered by the audit mandate. As noted earlier, SAIs may be enabled to audit government departments and statutory authorities through to the whole of government finances (that is, an 'ownership' mandate: Newberry and Pont-Newby, 2009). Coverage often also includes other entities and trusts that use public money, especially government-owned or -controlled entities, joint ventures and other affiliated entities. At the extreme, SAIs have a mandate to audit entities that are financially dependent on public resources, grant recipients and any that are recipients of public resources (Robertson, 2013). INTOSAI Principle 3 states that SAIs should be empowered to audit the use of all public money and resources by any beneficiary, regardless of the legal nature of that recipient, but there is wide variety in the ability or willingness of SAIs to apply that principle, both from a mandate and operational point of view (Robertson, 2013). The OECD (2014, p. 70) notes that the SAIs of both Chile and Israel play "an important role in the overall anti-corruption efforts in the public sector, including both prevention and detection of fraud and corruption". These are two countries that have made a choice to address this issue in consort with other public sector and autonomous institutions.

INTOSAI developed a full set of International Standards of Supreme Audit Institutions (ISSAIs) in 2010 at three different levels. Some SAIs follow all of these; others prefer to follow International Standards of Audit and/or standards they have set themselves. Such standards recommend communicating publicly the results of audits in order to exhibit public value and to maintain independence (Hay and Cordery, 2018). Barrett (1996) notes that accountability to citizens is crucial and must be combined with independence of funding and appointment. Accountability to citizens could be achieved through SAIs having strong relations with the media, although Bringselius (2014) warns that highlighting auditee failings through the media may impair auditor-auditee relationships. The Effective Institutions Platform (2014) states that SAI structure may be related to the way in which SAIs engage with the public, as well as the political and social context and the relative independence of the SAI.

It can be seen here that there is the possibility for wide diversity in the structure, mandate and operations of SAIs. They are important institutions and ones which have not been extensively studied or well understood. It is the purpose of this book to provide details on these aspects of SAIs in order to inform practitioners, students and researchers. We seek not only to outline reasons why public audit is undertaken and the variety of responses to this but also to frame how audit may develop in the future, given the current environment.

1.5 Overview and conclusion

This book is informed by a survey that was undertaken with the support of INTOSAI and elicited responses from 35 SAIs internationally. Each member of INTOSAI was contacted and asked to participate in the survey, and a link was sent through the Qualtrics online survey system. Regional INTOSAI organisations were advised of the survey which was made available only in English. The survey questions covered topics that are covered in Chapters 2–5.

First, in Chapter 2 we introduce neo-institutional theory and particularly how coercive, mimetic and normative isomorphism has been found in the spread of international accounting and auditing standards and how it has been applied to public sector audit. The chapter also analyses why public audit is undertaken. We take the classic explanations for audit in the private sector and apply them to public audit, along with the small amount of evidence to date of the usefulness of these explanations. We also reveal how SAIs currently perceive the demand for audit. Finally, we examine alternative explanations for public sector audit that have been put forward in prior literature.

Chapter 3 analyses the current context of audit, including explaining further the different structures, mandates and types of audit work that are undertaken internationally. We draw on a number of public sources to explain the diversity of structures, mandates and types of audit work undertaken. The survey we undertook provides supporting information in this respect. We examine arguments for isomorphism in these areas and the demand for audit.

In Chapter 4 we look to the future to analyse the risks and opportunities facing SAIs by an analysis of the global environment, future trends affecting governments, the accounting and auditing profession and public sector audit. New areas of audit will bring challenges and opportunities, and we discuss these in light of both our survey responses and the findings from the two prior chapters on isomorphism.

Chapter 5 concludes this book with an overview of the main themes, and findings that there is structural variety in SAIs but that this is impacted by isomorphic pressures. In addition, we find that the demands and reasons for audit are under-stated (and under-studied). Further, we suggest public sector audit continues to be valued and that the future is likely to see higher quality audits in this space due to the increase in accrual accounting and auditing standards. The realm of public sector audit is complex and demanding, and a Supreme Audit Institution appears to be an essential part of public administration systems. The aim of this book is to introduce research into SAIs and their activities, to explore the diversity of SAIs, their activities and the roles that they take on. We trust also that it will inspire further research into this fascinating area.

Notes

1 These are AFROSAI (African Organisation of Supreme Audit Institutions), ARABOSAI (Arab Organisation of Supreme Audit Institutions), ASOSAI (Asian Organisation of Supreme Audit Institutions), CAROSAI (Caribbean Organisation of Supreme Audit Institutions), EUROSAI (European Organisation of Supreme Audit Institutions), OLACEFS (Organisation of Latin American and Caribbean Supreme Audit Institutions) and PASAI (Pacific Association of Supreme Audit Institutions). AFROSAI also has two sub-groups, namely AFROSAI-E for the English-speaking African countries and CREFIAF representing the Francophone African countries.
2 Information downloaded from the internet: www.gov.uk/government/organisations/audit-commission.

References

Arthur *et al.* (2012) 'The user perspective in performance auditing: A case study of Norway', *American Journal of Evaluation*, 33(1), pp. 44–59. https://doi.org/10.1177/1098214011408283.

Barrett, P. (1996) 'Some thoughts about the roles, responsibilities and future scope of Auditors-General', *Australian Journal of Public Administration*, 55(4), pp. 137–146.

Barzelay, M. (1997) 'Central audit institutions and performance auditing: A comparative analysis of organizational strategies in the OECD', *Governance*, 10(3), pp. 235–260. https://doi.org/10.1111/0952-1895.411997041.

Bringselius, L. (2014) 'The dissemination of results from supreme audit institutions: Independent partners with the media?', *Financial Accountability & Management*, 30(1), pp. 75–95. https://doi.org/10.1111/faam.12028.

Clark, C. *et al.* (2007) 'Audit quality attributes of European Union supreme audit institutions', *European Business Review*, 19, pp. 40–71. https://doi.org/10.1108/09555340710714144.

Cordery, C. J. and Hay, D. (2018) 'Supreme audit institutions and public value: Demonstrating relevance', *Financial Accountability & Management*, 35(2), pp. 128–142.

Effective Institutions Platform (2014) *Supreme Audit Institutions and Stakeholder Engagement Practices: A Stocktaking Report*. Geneva: Effective Institutions Platform.

English, L. M. (2007) 'Performance audit of Australian public private partnerships: Legitimising government policies or providing independent oversight?', *Financial Accountability & Management*, 23(3), pp. 313–336. https://doi.org/10.1111/j.1468-0408.2007.00431.x.

Friedberg, A. and Lutrin, C. (2005) 'State audits in the United States, 1996–2000', *Journal of Public Budgeting, Accounting & Financial Management*, 17(1), pp. 1–32.

Funnell, W. (2015) 'Performance auditing and adjudicating political disputes', *Financial Accountability & Management*, 31(February), pp. 92–111. https://doi.org/10.1111/faam.12046.

Grimsey, D. and Lewis, M. K. (2005) 'Are public private partnerships value for money?: Evaluating alternative approaches and comparing academic and practitioner views', *Accounting Forum*, 29(4), pp. 345–378. https://doi.org/10.1016/j.accfor.2005.01.001.

Groenendijk, N. S. (2004) 'Assessing member states' management of EU finances: An empirical analysis of the annual reports of the European Court of Auditors, 1996–2001', *Public Administration*, 82(3), pp. 701–725. https://doi.org/10.1111/j.0033-3298.2004.00415.x.

Hay, D. and Cordery, C. J. (2018) 'The value of public sector audit: Literature and history', *Journal of Accounting Literature*. Elsevier, 40(June), pp. 1–15. https://doi.org/10.1016/j.acclit.2017.11.0010737-4607/.

International Organization of Supreme Audit Institutions (2004) 'Standards and guidelines for performance auditing based on INTOSAI's auditing standards and practical experience', *ISSAI 3000*. International Standards of Supreme Audit Institutions, pp. 1–76. Available at: The International Standards of Supreme Audit Institutions, ISSAI. https://www.issai.org/professional-pronouncements/?n=0-1000000000

Melo, M. A. *et al.* (2009) 'Political and institutional checks on corruption: Explaining the performance of Brazilian audit institutions', *Comparative Political Studies*, 42(9), pp. 1217–1244. https://doi.org/10.1177/0010414009331732.

Morin, D. (2011) 'Serving as magistrate at the French Cour des comptes: Navigating between tradition and modernity', *Accounting, Auditing & Accountability Journal*, 24(6), pp. 718–750. https://doi.org/10.1108/09513571111155528.

Morin, D. (2016) 'Democratic accountability during performance audits under pressure: A recipe for institutional hypocrisy?', *Financial Accountability & Management*, 32(February), pp. 104–124.

Mulgan, R. (2001) 'Auditors-General: Cuckoos in the managerialist nest?', *Australian Journal of Public Administration*, 60(2), pp. 24–34. https://doi.org/10.1111/1467-8500.00206.

Newberry, S. and Pont-Newby, S. (2009) 'Whole of government accounting in New Zealand: The ownership form of control', *Public Money & Management*, 29(4), pp. 235–242. https://doi.org/10.1080/09540960903035007.

OECD (2014) *Chile's Supreme Audit Institution: Enhancing Strategic Agility and Public Trust*. OECD Public Governance Reviews. Paris: OECD Publishing. http://doi.org/10.1787/9789264207561-en.

Paananen, M. (2016) 'Modified audit reports in the case of joint municipal authorities: Empirical evidence from Finland', *International Journal of Auditing*, 20(2), pp. 149–157. https://doi.org/10.1111/ijau.12062.

Pollitt, C. and Summa, H. (1997) 'Comparative and international administration reflexive watchdogs? How supreme audit institutions account for themselves', *Public Administration*, 75, pp. 313–336. https://doi.org/10.1111/1467-9299.00063.

Raudla, R. *et al.* (2016) 'The impact of performance audit on public sector organizations: The case of Estonia', *Public Organization Review*, 16(2), pp. 217–233. https://doi.org/10.1007/s11115-015-0308-0.

Reichborn-Kjennerud, K. (2013) 'Political accountability and performance audit: The case of the auditor general in Norway', *Public Administration*, 91(3), pp. 680–695. https://doi.org/10.1111/padm.12025.

Robertson, G. (2013) *Independence of Auditors General: A 2013 update of a survey of Australian and New Zealand legislation*. Victorian Auditor General's Office. Melbourne, Victoria, Australia.

Schelker, M. and Eichenberger, R. (2010) 'Auditors and fiscal policy: Empirical evidence on a little big institution', *Journal of Comparative Economics*. Association for Comparative Economic Studies, 38(4), pp. 357–380. https://doi.org/10.1016/j.jce.2010.09.002.

Shaoul, J. *et al*. (2008) 'The cost of using private finance to build, finance and operate hospitals', *Public Money & Management*, 28(2), pp. 101–108. https://doi.org/10.1111/j.1467-9302.2008.00628.x.

Sterck, M. and Bouckaert, G. (2006) 'International audit trends in the public sector', *Internal Auditor*, (August), pp. 49–53.

The World Bank (2001) 'Features and functions of supreme audit institutions', *From the Development Economics Vice Presidency and Poverty Reduction and Economic Management Network*, pp. 1–4. Available at: http://siteresources.worldbvank.org/INTLAWJUSTINST/Resources/premnote59.pdf.

2 Reasons for public audit and explanations for differences

2.1 Introduction

In this chapter we apply the existing research to analyse why public audit is undertaken and why it might vary from jurisdiction to jurisdiction. We draw upon institutional theory to explain the extent of variation, and the extent of similarity, among SAIs. We also take the classic explanations that are used to examine the value of auditing in the private sector and apply them to the public audit setting. We review the small amount of evidence available to date on the usefulness of these explanations in understanding SAIs. Further, we use data from our survey of SAIs to provide further evidence in this respect.

Explaining the similarities and differences among SAIs will be assisted by referring to how much they are similar to other SAIs, which is called the extent of their isomorphism. To examine this issue we apply neo-institutional theory, often just called institutional theory. Neo-institutional theory is well established and has been used in many organisational and accounting contexts. Organisations become similar to each other because of the effects of institutional forces from outside. It has been applied in explaining similar accounting issues such as the use of International Accounting Standards by a country or the auditing standards used in the private sector.

The value of auditing has been explained, especially in the private sector, using explanations drawn from economics. Hay and Cordery (2018) explore six explanations, namely agency, signalling, insurance, management control, governance and confirmation. Evidence from literature and history shows that the evidence is generally consistent with the agency and management control explanations. There is some support for signalling and insurance, but governance appears to have differing effects in the public sector. The confirmation hypothesis is potentially relevant but not yet investigated (Hay and Cordery, 2018, p. 1). The project reported in this book considers the extent to which data from the SAIs show support for both institutional theory and for the six explanations drawn from economics.

Another approach suitable to the public sector is Moore's model of public value (Cordery and Hay, 2018). The application of this model is also discussed.

Public sector accounting and auditing are known to be areas where the theory applied is diverse and some studies use no theory (Hay and Cordery, 2018, p. 2; Jacobs, 2012, p. 292; Modell, 2013, p. 104). We review the most widely cited studies. They suggest taking into account the constitutional position of SAIs; management trends in a country; cultural influences; legitimacy; and the use of the SAI as a legitimation device.

The sections in this chapter examine these sources of explanations for the differences and similarities among SAIs.

2.2 Neo-institutional theory

2.2.1 Neo-institutional theory definitions and discussions

Neo-institutional theory, based on a paper by DiMaggio and Powell (1983), helps to explain similarities and differences among organisations and their practices. It has been used to examine a wide range of business issues, including the adoption of International Accounting Standards by different countries (Judge *et al*., 2010). Institutions such as laws and regulations, and informal norms and conventions are the 'rules of the game' that influence what individuals and organisations do. DiMaggio and Powell (1983) argue that these institutions include three forces that make organisations similar to each other, namely coercive, mimetic and normative isomorphism. Organisations initially strive to become more effective, which may make them different from each other; at a later stage, they are influenced by a drive towards legitimacy, in which the three forces of isomorphism make them more similar to each other. Frumkin and Galaskiewicz (2004) suggest that public sector entities are more susceptible to institutional pressures than for-profit or not-for-profit entities. If that is the case, then greater isomorphism might also apply.

It is notable that many SAIs appear to have similar structures to each other. They tend to follow one of three or four models.[1] DiMaggio and Powell's (1983) model explaining why there are similarities among business organisations may be helpful in explaining why SAIs resemble each other. They start with the observation that many business organisations are similar to each other. They suggest that organisations in an early stage of their life cycle display considerable diversity, but once they become well established, there are forces that push them towards homogenisation, not necessarily for greater efficiency but in order to achieve legitimacy (DiMaggio and Powell, 1983). "Organizations compete for political power and institutional legitimacy, for social as well as economic fitness" (DiMaggio and Powell, 1983, p. 150). One of the examples they use is that of civil service reform in the United States (DiMaggio and Powell, 1983). DiMaggio and Powell (1983, p. 149) call the process that forces organisations to resemble each other "isomorphism". The three mechanisms through which isomorphism occurs are:

> 1) coercive isomorphism that stems from political influences and the problem of legitimacy; 2) mimetic isomorphism resulting from standard responses to uncertainty; and 3) normative isomorphism associated with professionalization.
>
> (DiMaggio and Powell, 1983, p. 150)

The three types intermingle in empirical settings, but they tend to derive from different conditions and they lead to different outcomes (DiMaggio and Powell, 1983). Although legitimacy is associated with coercive isomorphism, legitimacy is also mentioned as a factor driving mimetic and normative isomorphism (DiMaggio and Powell, 1983).

In further discussion, DiMaggio and Powell (1983) observe that coercive isomorphism may be felt as force to adopt a government mandate, such as preparing accounts, but also more subtly through interactions with other organisations, such as donors. Mimetic processes occur when, in times of uncertainty, organisations model themselves on other organisations that they perceive to be legitimate or successful. Normative pressures come primarily from professionalisation, both as a result of formal education and of legitimation in a cognitive base produced by university specialists; and professional networks across which new models can spread (DiMaggio and Powell, 1983). In the public sector, parliamentary criticism means these entities are likely to follow recommended practice to maintain legitimacy (James and John, 2007; Keerasuntonpong and Cordery, 2018). Thus, they are likely to increase bureaucracy (Frumkin and Galaskiewicz, 2004). DiMaggio and Powell (1983) predict that there will be greater similarity to other organisations because of coercive isomorphism when there is greater dependence on another organisation or greater centralisation of its resource supply. SAIs play a coercive role for the public sector entities that they oversee, as they scrutinise and review public sector accountability (Mulgan, 1997)

Organisations will be more likely to model themselves on other organisations because of mimetic isomorphism when there is more uncertainty of the relationship between means and ends and when the goals of an organisation are uncertain (DiMaggio and Powell, 1983). Organisations will become more like other organisations in the same field because of normative isomorphism when there is greater participation of its managers in trade or professional organisations. Keerasuntonpong and Cordery (2018), in a study of SAIs' influence on local government reporting, did not find evidence of normative isomorphism, but little other research exists on SAIs' normative impact.

DiMaggio and Powell (1983) also propose hypotheses about organisational fields. They predict that there will be more isomorphism when the organisational field depends on a single source of support or when agencies transact with state agencies. The fewer the number of visible alternative organisational models in the field, the faster the rate of isomorphism (p. 155). Further, they predict that greater uncertainty of technology, or greater ambiguity of goals within a field, will be associated with a greater rate of isomorphic change. They also predicted that the greater the extent of Professionalisation in a field, and the greater the extent of structuration, the greater the degree of isomorphic changes and isomorphism (DiMaggio and Powell, 1983).[2] DiMaggio and Powell's model is summarised in Table 2.1.

Applying the broad outline of DiMaggio and Powell's (1983) model to SAIs, we might expect SAIs to be structured similarly in these circumstances:

- If it is the case that SAIs are dependent on another organisation, especially the state, for funding.
- When there is uncertainty about how to achieve the objectives of auditing; when goals are uncertain.
- When managers are professional and engage in professional organisations.
- When there are few visible alternative models.

These circumstances each appear to be very likely to apply to most SAIs. If so, then we can predict that these influences will be evident in the nature of the SAIs in each country. This issue is explored in Chapter 3.

Table 2.1 Isomorphism (DiMaggio and Powell, 1983)

Mechanism	*Source of pressure*	*Circumstances when relevant*
Coercive isomorphism	Force applied by government or interactions with other organisations	Dependence on another organisation
Mimetic isomorphism	Copying successful or legitimate organisations	Uncertain relationships between means and ends, or uncertain goals
Normative isomorphism	Professionalism from education or from networks	Managers participate in professional organisations

SAIs are generally funded by government, or by the legislature directly, and they transact extensively with state agencies, so that isomorphism might be expected to occur to a relatively greater extent. On the other hand, there are a number of different models in use by various SAIs, and this might inhibit isomorphism. The activities of SAIs are highly professional, and their managers tend to take part in activities such as those of regional SAIs and INTOSAI. The extent of this activity should also contribute to isomorphism.

2.2.2 Institutional theory applied to accounting standards

Neo-institutional theory has been applied to examine an issue in accounting that has some parallels to public sector auditing, namely the adoption of International Financial Reporting Standards (IFRS) by different economies (Judge *et al.*, 2010). Judge *et al.* (2010) concluded that institutional theory was well supported by the data about IFRS. The support included evidence that each of the three forms of isomorphism described in institutional theory were relevant in explaining which countries had adopted IFRS and the importance of legitimacy in the process of adoption. Judge *et al.* (2010, p. 151) observed, "the key assumption within institutional theory is that all social actors are seeking legitimacy, and/or reinventing legitimacy norms, within the institutional environment". There is a well-established international movement towards harmonisation of financial reporting standards. Some economies have adopted IFRS more quickly than others, and institutional theory provided an explanation why.

Judge *et al.* (2010) were able to explain the considerable variation in adoption of IFRS by reference to three variables: foreign aid, import penetration, and education, with controls for market capitalisation and GDP growth. Their analysis proceeded by examining three hypotheses. One related to each of coercive, mimetic and normative isomorphism. The three types of isomorphism were operationalised as:

> Coercive: Coercive institutions can force an economy to conform to international norms and standards. Their hypothesis argues that external political and economic pressures are coercive pressure. An example is foreign aid from institutions like the International Monetary Fund, or other non-governmental organizations.
>
> (Judge *et al.*, 2010, p. 163)

> Mimetic: Individuals, organizations and nations tend to mimic others who are regarded as successful. Economies that are open to foreign trade expose firms to a wide range of "best practices" which firms are

> likely to adopt. They hypothesize that IFRS adoption will be associated with economies that are globally integrated.
>
> (Judge *et al.*, 2010, p. 164)

> Normative: professional norms can lead to adoption of conformity of thought, and are more likely to be influential when there is a high degree of professional technical knowledge. They expected that greater educational advancement would be associated with adoption of IFRS.
>
> (Judge *et al.*, 2010, p. 164)

In each case, they considered a number of variables to measure these influences. The variables tended to be subject to collinearity with each other, and the authors chose foreign aid, import penetration and percentage of the population enrolled in secondary schools as the respective measures for the three types of isomorphism. They included relative capital market size and GDP growth as control variables (Judge *et al.*, 2010).

Judge *et al.* (2010) examined 132 countries. Their results show an adjusted R-squared of 21%, and they found significant results for the three isomorphism measures. The results for foreign aid are weak (significant at the 0.10 level), but there is stronger support for the other two measures (Judge *et al.*, 2010, p. 167). Judge *et al.* (2010) also considered it appropriate to repeat their tests with 23 countries excluded because each was subject to a specific influence. The results with these observations excluded were more significant. However, the reasons for the exclusions are somewhat subjective (e.g. "strong domestic GAAP" for New Zealand).

Judge *et al.* (2010) also took into account other well-known variables representing differences among countries including Hofstede's (1980, 2001) cultural dimensions and La Porta *et al.*'s (2006) securities law-related factors. Judge *et al.* (2010) examined models with these measures as control variables. The additional variables were not significant, but some of the other variables lost some of their significance and the overall explanatory power of the models was less. Other than these measures, they did not examine the legal system of the countries or their historical influences.

The study is not a very strong explanation for differences among countries, but it helps to explain the differences to some extent. It provides a perspective for the (normative) point of view that the authors attribute to many policy makers, namely that all countries should adopt best practice. National institutions may help this kind of harmonisation, but they are also capable of blocking it. Judge *et al.* (2010) invite other researchers to adopt their framework.

The control variables examined by Judge *et al.* (2010) for cultural factors and securities law will also be helpful in understanding SAIs.

There are other papers that are not entirely supportive of institutional theory in this setting. Christensen (2005) undertook a qualitative study of the adoption of (for-profit) accrual accounting by the Australian public sector, finding that mimetic pressures were chiefly responsible for this homogenisation. On the contrary, Pilcher's (2011) survey suggests coercive isomorphism caused Australian local governments to take up IFRS. This is in concordance with Carpenter and Feroz (2001) in the US public sector. However, Oulasvirta (2014) found in the Finnish economy that governmental accounting culture is deeply rooted, and pressures to change are heartily resisted. In our application of the theory we also consider these potential contrary influences.

2.2.3 Institutional theory and auditing standards

There is a study applying neo-institutional theory to changes in auditing standards (Baker *et al.*, 2014). The study examined private sector auditing standards – which are often also an influence on the standards applied by SAIs. They examined three countries: the US, France and Canada. The system of auditor regulation in these three countries (and others around the world) is becoming more uniform. Baker *et al.* concluded that the substantial changes in each country were driven by pressures for regulators and professionals to enhance their legitimacy and that changes were made that "give the appearance of institutional isomorphism" (Baker *et al.*, 2014, p. 374). The reforms in the United States that were made in the Sarbanes-Oxley Act in 2001, after scandals such as Enron, were driven by external forces and were thus described by Baker *et al.* (2014) as an example of coercive isomorphism. There were no similar scandals in France, but changes were made to make the regulatory structure for auditors appear similar to that in the US, an example of mimetic isomorphism. There were also no similar scandals in Canada, but changes were made with influence from the auditing profession, and those can be seen as normative isomorphism (Baker *et al.*, 2014).

2.2.4 Institutional theory and SAIs

A study comparing institutions in Finland and Norway by Johnsen *et al.* (2001) uses a framework of neo-institutional theory. They conclude that variations in the use of value for money auditing are influenced by differences in management and by mimetic isomorphism related to the uncertain and ambiguous environments in which the local governments they studied operate (Johnsen *et al.*, 2001).[3]

Christensen (2003) argues that adoption of the commercial model of accounting in the public sector is also driven by mimetic isomorphism because of the use of consultants who were familiar with private sector models. He argues this was particularly due to goal ambiguity, lack of technological understanding and an uncertain environment, factors suggested by DiMaggio and Powell as contributing to mimetic isomorphism (Christensen, 2005). We suggest that the influence of professional consultants could also be depicted as a source of normative isomorphism.

A related area, that of a Public Accounts Committee of Parliament (in Bangladesh) has been examined by Khan and Hoque (2016). They applied institutional theory and found that these bodies of governmental accountability are influenced by coercive isomorphism via international donor agencies, mimetic isomorphism in which they copied the model of Parliaments such as those of Australia, Canada and the UK, and normative isomorphism which reached them through an international training programme in Australia (Khan and Hoque, 2016). Agency costs (discussed in a later section of this chapter) also had an impact.

Chan *et al.* (2016) examine Samoa and Tonga; and using the framework of Clark and De Martinis (2003), find that accountability is influenced by NPM and earlier British history. Small isolated developing nations are expected to be influenced by neighbouring developed countries and by their former colonisers. Samoa depends heavily on private remittances and on foreign aid. It has a traditional government system including traditional family leaders (matai) and village councils, plus a Westminster parliamentary democracy. Tonga also receives a large proportion of its GDP from private remittances and foreign aid. It was never colonised and has a constitutional monarchy, with more centralised control than in Samoa. The paper draws on DiMaggio and Powell. The paper proceeds to examine the institution of the auditor-general (AG) in each country, including a framework of the powers of Parliament, oversight of the auditor-general, funding, mandate to perform audits and independence from Parliament. Chan *et al.* (2016) observe that there have been recent changes that make the AG in each country more similar to that in "the Clark and De Martinis ideal" and "the Commonwealth law closest to them". The authors (Chan *et al.*, 2016) describe the changes as mimetic. Despite these influences, both audit bodies in Samoa and Tonga concentrate heavily on compliance auditing (verifying of individual payments), and as a result, there are few resources for audits of financial reporting or for performance auditing. In any case, the study reports that financial statements are often more than a year late, so that financial report auditing would be of less value.

Heald (2018), while observing that public auditing is under-theorised, also observes that in many cases former colonies have adopted an SAI model similar to their former colonising power. He regards this, especially in countries that are only weakly democratic, as "mimetic isomorphism without regard to context" (Heald, 2018, p. 1). Heald (2018) also examines arguments about transparency and trust, proposing that greater transparency can undermine trust.

A recent study on SAIs and corruption (Reichborn-Kjennerud *et al*., 2019) appears to suggest that coercive, mimetic and normative pressures result in SAIs appearing ineffective in combatting corruption. They conclude that the way SAIs combat corruption is not related to the extent of corruption in a country but by an interaction with coercive, mimetic and normative pressures. The study examines seven diverse countries in Europe and Africa. They observe that coercive pressures from the political system within a country can lead to sanctions against an SAI when it fights corruption, even when there are high expectations from the public that the SAI will do so. They also observe that mimetic isomorphism applies, where countries will follow models from other countries, and also note the risk that this will lead to models being adopted that "make sense in one context [being] transferred uncritically to another", for example, from a country with low levels of corruption to one with high levels (Reichborn-Kjennerud *et al*., 2019, p. 4). They also observe normative pressures from professional accountants, including that private sector auditors "define themselves away" from responsibilities involving corruption (Reichborn-Kjennerud *et al*., 2019, p. 5).

2.2.5 Summary

The model developed by DiMaggio and Powell (1983) provides a useful source to explain why organisations become similar. The forces are relevant to SAIs, and previous studies have used their approach effectively in accounting settings and the public sector. We might therefore expect that isomorphism will be important in explaining SAI structures, depending on the extent to which there is dependence on another organisation, the degree of uncertainty and whether SAI managers are part of a professional network.

2.3 Explanations previously applied to auditing

There are several widely used explanations for the value of auditing that have been applied in previous research, mainly in the private sector. Hay and Cordery (2018) applied six explanations (agency, signalling, insurance, management control, governance and confirmation) to ways in which public sector auditing can be expected to be valuable. They found that the explanations were generally helpful in explaining public sector auditing, although some issues required further investigation.

2.3.1 Agency theory

The agency theory explanation for auditing is that auditing is valuable because it reduces agency costs. This is the agency theory explanation for the value of auditing. Agency relationships apply where one party, the principal, delegates control over resources to another, the agent (Wallace, 1980). This is often between a shareholder and manager, but agency relationships also apply widely in the public sector. When there are agency relationships, there are costs. Agents might spend money for their own benefit; or might shirk their duties; or might be diligent but misguided. Because of these risks, the principal will be less inclined to enter into a relationship with an agent. Agents will want to prevent that from happening and might try to prevent it by reducing the costs of monitoring. One way to reduce monitoring costs is by appointing an auditor to report on the financial statements. This is likely to be an efficient approach when there is one agent (a manager or chief executive) and multiple principals (such as shareholders, or cabinet, Parliament and voters). There is evidence that audits have been voluntarily arranged for these reasons in some circumstances (Wallace, 1980; Chow, 1982). A partner in the US firm of KPMG wrote that "auditing adds tremendous value" because of the way it can reduce agency costs and lead to a lower cost of capital (Elliott, 1994).

Agency theory has been used to explain issues related to financial reporting and auditing in previous public sector studies (Baber, 1983; Bradbury and Scott, 2015; Jensen, 2005). "Politicians are the elected agents of the electorate and hence an agency problem exists", according to Zimmerman (1977, p. 118). Agency relationships in the public sector are more complex than in the private sector as there are several levels of relationship (Streim, 1994). A relevant quote by Moe (1984, p. 765) states that:

> Democratic politics are easily viewed in principal-agent terms. Citizens are principals, politicians are their agents. Politicians are principals, bureaucrats are their agents. The whole of politics is therefore structured by a chain of principal-agent relationships, from citizen to politician to bureaucratic subordinate and on down the hierarchy to the lowest-level bureaucrats who actually deliver services to citizens.

Thus, agency relationships in the public sector are more complicated than those in the private sector. There are agency relationships between voters (as principals) and politicians (as agents); between government and Parliament; and between government and public servants. Hay (2001) shows that accountability can be linked to the extent of decentralisation of an activity and that the extent of decentralisation is related to the knowledge transfer costs and extent of dependence associated with a public sector activity (Hay, 2003).

Blume and Voigt (2011) use an agency model to assess the economic effects of differences in SAIs among 40 countries. Blume and Voigt (2011) develop measures of the mandate of the SAI (financial auditing or performance auditing, public reporting), its independence and institutional environment. Independence includes a measure of financial independence (the resources allocated to auditing measured by the number of SAI staff in relation to the country's population), and institutional environment including whether the SAI uses the Napoleonic or court system as opposed to the alternatives of the Westminster system or the board system. Control variables are included for GDP, trade, civil liberties, proportion of the population over 65, ethnolinguistic fractionalisation and the Protestant religion. The dependent variables include measures of fiscal policy, government effectiveness and corruption, and productivity. Their auditing data is drawn from surveys by the World Bank and by INTOSAI. There are very few significant results. The differences among SAIs do not seem to have any effect on the dependent variables selected. The only exception is that countries using the court system are associated with greater corruption (Blume and Voigt, 2011).

There appears to be potential for extensions to the approach in Blume and Voigt (2011). These should include considering a wider range of explanatory variables for national culture and accounting, control variables for other institutional features that might affect the outputs and more precise measures of what it is that SAIs might have an impact on. Blume and Voigt (2011, p. 226) suggest that a better measure of "factual independence" of an SAI would be desirable (compared to their measure, the number of employees in proportion to inhabitants).

Some public sector auditing research using agency theory is consistent with agency theory as used in mainstream research (Johnsen *et al.*, 2001; Jacobs, 2012). Other research uses theories less likely to be found in mainstream auditing such as governmentality based on Foucault's work (Jacobs, 2012).

Power's thesis of the "Audit Society" (Power, 2003) and related works by Power are noted as an example of "the closest thing to theory indigenous in the accounting literature" (Jacobs, 2012, p. 18).

Hay and Cordery (2018) conclude that the agency explanation is the most widely researched approach in both private sector and public sector settings. However, there is scope to apply it to understand public sector auditing in various jurisdictions (Cordery and Hay, 2018).

2.3.2 The signalling explanation

Under the signalling explanation, managers have better information about the value and quality of their business than outside investors do (Wallace, 1980). This is 'information asymmetry'. The managers can add credibility to statements in the financial report and increase the value of their business by engaging a higher quality auditor (Titman and Trueman, 1986). Research on signalling has been applied to public sector accounting and auditing in studies like Evans and Patton (1987) and Sanders and Allen (1993) which examine whether public sector entities that apply for certification of their financial statements do so in accordance with the incentives for signalling. Both find support for the signalling explanation. James and John (2007) also found a role for the UK Audit Commission in being an independent public body, bringing together a bundle of measures of local government performance to provide voters with an overall assessment of service performance and management competence.

A related question is examined by Lamoreaux *et al.* (2015), namely whether the amount of international development aid loans provided by the World Bank to a country is related to the quality of its accounting. They find that development aid loans are higher for countries with stronger accounting quality, where IFRS use is mandated and where the audit environment is stronger. This evidence appears to support the signalling explanation. However, this result only applies to countries that have relatively high corruption levels. Further, the World Bank appears to overlook accounting and audit quality in countries where geo-political interests are relatively aligned with those of the US.

Hay and Cordery (2018) suggest that a potentially interesting research question is whether governments provide signalling via better auditing, and whether such signals could have an effect on interest rates or foreign investment in the country.

2.3.3 Insurance

The insurance explanation suggests that stakeholders may want audits because the audits might provide a chance of recovering certain types of losses. The auditor can be perceived as a target that can be sued to recover any investment losses because the auditor has "deep pockets" (Chow, 1982). As a result, auditors can find themselves facing costly litigation even when they have little responsibility for the losses.

Wallace (1980) suggests that an audit in the public sector can provide "political insurance" whereby governments can blame auditors for failings by public sector managers. Hay and Cordery (2018) consider that the insurance explanation is relevant and plausible in the public sector, but more investigation is needed as evidence outside New Zealand is sparse. There is some overlap between the agency, signalling and insurance explanations, and the three explanations frequently work together.

2.3.4 The management control explanation

Sometimes business owners purchase voluntary audits as part of a control system within their organisation. Management control for the benefit of internal management is another explanation for auditing. The public sector equivalent to this explanation would occur when executive government or high-level bureaucrats demand an audit to assist with the control over a government entity. Abdel-khalik (1993) showed that private companies are more likely to voluntarily choose to have an audit when they have more layers of hierarchy or are larger (Abdel-khalik, 1993). Auditing helps top management to control complex organisations in the public sector as well as in private entities. It might be expected that there would be an association between circumstances when there is large size, complexity or decentralisation and greater use of auditing (Hay and Cordery, 2018, p. 7).

2.3.5 Governance

Better corporate governance is not a substitute for auditing but is complementary to it. The demand for auditing is higher when there are other governance mechanisms in place. There is a tendency for governance to be enhanced in recent times in both the private and public sectors, and this is usually associated with greater demand for auditing. Bédard and Compernolle (2014, pp. 256–259) review research showing that stronger audit committees are associated with choosing higher quality auditors, greater control over the risk of non-audit services and increased negotiating power for auditors compared to managers.

However, it may be that corporate governance relationships work differently in the public sector. Botica Redmayne *et al.* (2011) shows that audit committees in the public sector were associated with higher audit fees for profit-oriented public sector entities, and lower audit fees for public benefit public sector entities (Botica Redmayne *et al.*, 2011). The suggestions that improved governance has a different effect in the public sector compared to the private sector is worth further investigation (Hay and Cordery, 2018, p. 7).

2.3.6 The confirmation hypothesis

Under the confirmation hypothesis, announcements about past financial performance and position are important because they verify earlier unaudited announcements. Announcements by companies, such as profit announcements, contain information that has mostly been reflected already in share prices. This finding by Ball and Brown (1968) has been well documented.

As a result, audited announcements of financial information usually do not add as much information as announcements of new, price-sensitive information (Ball and Brown, 1968). Ball *et al.* (2012) suggest that "audited financial reporting and voluntary disclosure of managers' private information are complementary mechanisms for communicating with investors, not substitutes" and that "managers are encouraged to be more truthful when they are aware their disclosures of private information subsequently will be confirmed". The confirmation hypothesis suggests that while voluntary announcements of private information held by managers have market impact, they are complements to subsequent audit financial reports. The confirmation hypothesis is plausible in understanding why auditing is important even when unaudited announcements are widely used, and unaudited information often has more impact. In the public sector, unaudited information is also often important, so that there are potential research opportunities (Hay and Cordery, 2018, p. 7).

2.3.7 How do these explanations 'fit' with SAIs' views?

As noted in Chapter 1, this book is informed by a survey that was undertaken with the support of INTOSAI and elicited responses from 35 SAIs internationally. Each of the widely used explanations in the prior subsections 2.3.1 to 2.3.6 was expressed in the survey, and SAIs were asked to select as many or few that were relevant to why stakeholders demand audit. The results are provided in Figure 2.1.[4] (The responses were received from SAIs across the spectrum of different types as discussed further in Chapter 3.)

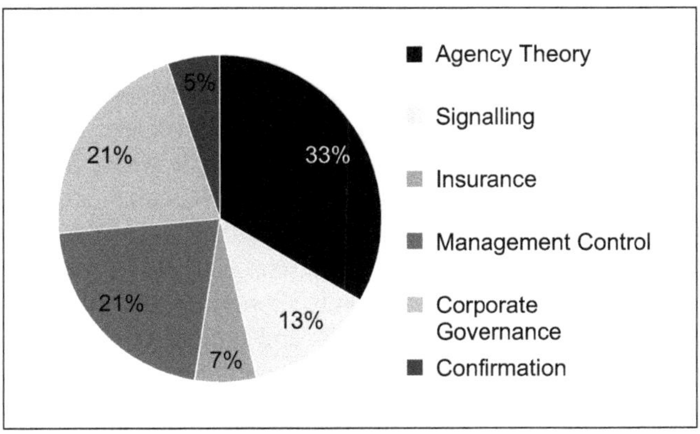

Figure 2.1 SAIs' beliefs as to why stakeholders demand audit

In strong confirmation of agency theory, comments added by SAIs included that they believe that:

> disclosure of audit results will increase the fairness and the use of public resources by managers.
>
> . . . Parliament want an audit because it is constitutionally holding the Government of the day to account.

Nevertheless, the use of public audit for management control and corporate governance were also strongly supported. This is likely in decentralised situations (which frequently occur in the public sector). As noted previously, the corporate governance explanation is one that deserves further study. Demand from stakeholders for audit as a signalling mechanism had less support from SAIs and even less still, the role of the insurance and confirmation hypotheses. Nevertheless, all of the explanations had some support.

The notion that stakeholders would be within the same country is also challenged by responses such as:

> donors and international agencies are demanding oversight and accountability.

There was a strong emphasis in the extra comments on stakeholders' demands for value for money and performance issues to 'ensure best use is made of public funds'. This links to the need to consider public value and how SAIs assist in the delivery of that.

2.4 Public value examined using Moore's model

Cordery and Hay (2018) examine the components of public value delivered by SAIs and analyse how SAIs report on their delivery of public value. Public value is seen as having a utilitarian ideal of effectiveness and efficiency, and a deontological aim of achieving a just and fair society. The study uses Moore's (1995, 2013) model of the strategic triangle where public entities build value through strategic development of public value, ensuring legitimacy and support and building from operating capacity. These factors are in turn made up of two sub-factors each: ensuring public sector accountability and independently and objectively supporting reform; SAI independence and building trust; and high quality and audit and responsiveness and voice. These factors and sub-factors are supported by reference to existing research.

Cordery and Hay (2018) then measure SAI reporting (in English) on public value for 24 measures applied to 16 SAIs. Countries in the Commonwealth and the US scored substantially more highly than non-English-speaking countries. They conclude that while SAIs report on their utilitarian goals of increasing effectiveness and efficiency, they do not critique or build fairness and justice in society. This issue is another area where there is potential for further research.

2.5 Explanations and evidence from other previous studies

There are other previous studies that examine SAIs more specifically and that use a variety of theoretical approaches. The most cited studies of SAIs according to González-Díaz and García-Fernández (2017) are seven papers discussed in this section (Gupta *et al.*, 1994; Barzelay, 1997; Pollitt and Summa, 1997; Basu *et al.*, 1999; Broadbent and Laughlin, 2003; Pollitt, 2003; Skærbæk, 2009). These studies contribute to understanding SAIs in different ways. They make use of neo-institutional theory and other theories (especially agency theory) to varying extents.

Reviewing those highly cited papers in chronological order shows that government structure and institutions were often important influences.

Gupta *et al.* (1994) apply institutional theory and contingency theory to the activities of the General Accounting Office (GAO) in the United States. They observe that institutional forces are known to be most powerful in government and professional settings. Institutional theory is relevant because entities like SAIs gain legitimacy from conforming to external expectations. It may be that organisations will adopt bureaucratic controls for symbolic purposes while actually relying on other forms of control. Contingency theory implies that members of an organisation will perform at their best when the form of coordination and control coincides with the work processes, especially the task uncertainty of the work processes. The theories interact. Gupta *et al.* (1994) conduct a questionnaire study and find support for the propositions they examine, including the use of more bureaucratic control in more institutionalised contexts and more personal and group modes of control when there is greater task difficulty.

Barzelay (1997) compares performance auditing among SAIs in Sweden, Germany, France, the UK, the US and Canada. The paper mentions the influence of neo-institutional theory but does not explore it further. Barzelay argues that variations in performance auditing depend on the relationship between the executive and the legislature, not on how the SAI is positioned. In some cases, there is a powerful entity with which the SAI has an intense client relationship, and in these cases, performance auditing flourishes (Barzelay, 1997).

Pollitt and Summa (1997) observed that there are considerable differences among SAIs. They examined the specific examples of the UK, France, Sweden, Finland and the European Court of Auditors, examining in particular what the SAIs reported about their own efficiency and effectiveness, and the extent to which they were influenced by the New Public Management (NPM). They suggested that the differences may be related to differing constitutional positions or administrative cultures of the SAIs.[5] They found that the subset of SAIs that they examined fell into two camps: the Finnish, Swedish and UK SAIs in one group and the French and European bodies in the other. The former group made a point of presenting information about their performance to the general public, which Pollitt and Summa (1997) describe as the managerialist approach. The second camp takes a constitutionalist approach, reporting on their findings and not on their own performance, as they rely on their constitutional status instead of their results. Pollitt and Summa (1997) perceive the managerialist approach as mirroring the extent of the influence of NPM in each country. They also argue that the different constitutional position of the SAIs affects the extent to which they are susceptible to management 'fashions'. This view seems consistent with mimetic isomorphism. They suggest that cultural influences, such as transparency and openness, are also significant.

Basu *et al.* (1999) examine the activities of the US GAO. They consider the issue of the complex interconnections between the work done by the organisation and the image presented, and conclude that the two are not decoupled or tightly coupled, but that loose coupling applies. The GAO's reports contain both symbolic and technical properties. The contents of the report are important to maintain the legitimacy of the GAO. Institutional theory is relevant because the survival of an organisation depends on its conforming to social norms. They observe that the GAO avoids criticising policy but concentrates on its implementation. They also report how the GAO was criticised by the minority party (the Republicans) as being a "lackey" for the Democrats (Basu *et al.*, 1999, p. 516) and that when the Republicans later gained a majority that the GAO's budget and staffing were reduced (Basu *et al.*, 1999, p. 517). The GAO closely monitored press coverage of its activities, and the extent of coverage influenced the priority of which activities were carried out. The strength of the connections between the work done and the image presented depends on the relative power of the various constituents, such as Congress, the press, the public and the agencies audited, with Congress having the most power and the agencies that are audited having the least.

Broadbent and Laughlin (2003) examine how governments control a large part of society and that SAIs provide legitimation of government activities. They portray the function of SAIs as providing legitimation "partly to avoid the searching questions from the public" (Broadbent and Laughlin, 2003). They examine the private finance initiative in the UK. They use an underlying framework of agency theory and distinguish between political accountability and managerial accountability. The auditor can investigate or challenge any policy objectives but operates self-imposed constraints to avoid "enraging" the government (Broadbent and Laughlin, 2003, p. 34). While independent bodies exist to provide an independent check, they do not, and instead provide legitimisation of government activities (Broadbent and Laughlin, 2003, p. 44).

Pollitt (2003) examines the strategic choices made in performance auditing by six European SAIs and the extent of change and convergence. He observes common trends and convergence. Changes were driven by a common set of external influences, especially from management reform, and the mandates of the SAIs can be seen as being in a constant state of flux.[6] Regarding independence, Pollitt (2003) concludes that the bodies are indeed independent: "It is hard to see these august bodies, all of them protected by high levels of statutory independence, as no more than passive pawns in the wider political game". (Pollitt does not make reference to Broadbent and Laughlin (2003) or their argument that SAIs are not independent watchdogs but instead providers of legitimacy.)

Skærbæk (2009) examines the military forces in Denmark and the manoeuvring by auditor and auditee for the auditor to become involved in performance auditing. The state auditors had expertise and were able to use it, but doing so required the auditors to develop a strategy and be recognised as "central in performance measurement" (Skærbæk, 2009) as well as manoeuvring by the auditors. The auditors were able to legitimise these public sector activities.

Research by (Morin, 2001, 2014) is also widely cited. Morin (2001) examined whether value for money audits result in long-term improvements and examined the factors that contributed to audits that result in improvements. She concluded that is not known whether the recommendations of value for money auditors are followed or not and whether they lead to improvements anyway (Morin, 2001). In some cases, the audits serve no purpose for taxpayers except "to lull them with illusions that things will improve" (Morin, 2001, p. 116). In a later study, she concluded that "auditors do exert an influence on the organizations audited, but their influence attempts fail fairly often" (Morin, 2014, p. 421). Her conclusions appear consistent with other findings that auditing can simply provide legitimisation (Broadbent and Laughlin, 2003).

Yamamoto and Kim (2019) apply an "institution approach" to comparing the SAIs of Japan and Korea, under which the SAI is expected to adapt to their institutional role. The two SAIs have different roles. In Japan, the SAI mainly contributes to the needs of Ministers and Cabinet; while in Korea there is a wider range of stakeholders, the National Assembly, the public and the president or the executive (Yamamoto and Kim, 2019).

A review of recent public sector auditing research, and the development of research over time, is provided by Johnsen (2019). Johnsen explains that New Public Management and "the audit society" are useful in explaining the development of audit institutions over recent decades and the expanded audit activities being carried out. (This development is also seen by Pollitt and Summa (1997) and Pollitt (2003).) The NPM emphasises transparency and accountability, and the measurement of outputs and outcomes (Hood, 1995; Johnsen, 2019). The "audit society" is a depiction of increased demand for auditing and activities similar to auditing in an "audit explosion" (Power, 1997; Johnsen, 2019).

A recent literature review (Bonollo, 2019) examines research on the outcomes of SAIs. It considers 40 papers and reports a predominance of Scandinavian studies. Bonollo (2019) recognises four types of SAIs, namely Westminster, board, Napoleonic and an auditor-general within the government structure. Most papers examine a single country; they tend to use qualitative methods and examine perceptions. Bonollo (2019) sees that approach as more suitable to examining performance audits. She also refers to significant changes being made to SAIs as part of NPM. She observes that some studies perceive increased emphasis on auditing as positive (Barzelay, 1997), while others see it as negative (Power, 1997), viz: the 'audit explosion'. She argues that more research is needed on audits of traditional financial reporting and on a wider range of countries, especially those using the Napoleonic model.

The group of papers discussed in this section provides some further issues to be considered in the data collection and analysis for this study. These issues are complementary to the theory discussed in the earlier parts of the chapter. Based on these widely cited papers, we should expect to find that the position and activities of an SAI are influenced by:

- Its constitutional position (Pollitt and Summa, 1997) and the relationship between executive and legislature (Barzelay, 1997).
- Management trends, influences and fashions, especially New Public Management (Pollitt and Summa, 1997; Pollitt, 2003) and perhaps including the 'audit society' (Jacobs, 2012; Johnsen, 2019).
- Cultural influences (Pollitt and Summa, 1997).
- The legitimacy of the SAI including institutional theory (Gupta *et al.*, 1994; Basu *et al.*, 1999).
- The use of the SAI as a device for legitimation of government activities (Broadbent and Laughlin, 2003; Morin, 2014).

2.6 Discussion and conclusion

It has been apparent for many years that public sector auditing is under-researched (e.g. Banker *et al.*, 1992) and recently Johnsen (2019) observed that "There has been, and still is, a need for more evidence on the workings and impacts of audit in the public sector in different accountability regimes and in different countries and for different stake-holders". Nevertheless, there is a substantial body of research, which we have discussed.

Hay and Cordery (2018) concluded that there are specific areas in which further research will be productive, including comparative studies of Supreme Audit Institutions and their impact. They also argue for reconciliation of the differences between the two major areas of research, the alternative and the mainstream; and more extensive examination of the demand for value for money auditing. They observe that it is not well documented just how much public sector auditing varies among countries and comment:

> We observe that it is not well-documented just how much public sector auditing varies among countries. In discussing issues with public sector auditors and researchers, we found that the full extent of variations among jurisdictions was often not appreciated.
>
> (Hay and Cordery, 2018, p. 12)

The research discussed so far suggests how to develop further our understanding of SAIs. We can expect SAIs to be influenced by sociological isomorphism, influenced by coercive, mimetic and normative factors that might include for example international funding sources, trade partners and professional activities; and by economic influences such as agency costs and the other commonly used economic explanations. The structure of the government institutions, including the SAI, the adoption of new management trends and the legitimation of government expenditure are other epxalantions that have been provided. These explanations could be subsumed under agency theory and institutional theory, but they are important enough to require additonal consideration. Therefore, we proceed by examining SAIs with reference to theory.

We expect to see variation among SAIs, with a trend to isomorphism. Isomorphism can be applied in different ways, and a wide range of external factors have been considered as influences. We should expect the influence of structural factors about the type of SAI; economic explanations, especially agency theory; and the presence of legitimation.

Notes

1 Three in the World Bank model (Stapenhurst and Titsworth, 2001); four in Pollitt and Summa (1997) and Bonollo (2019); two according to Reichborn-Kjennerud et al. (2019). These models are examined in Chapter 3.
2 Structuration is discussed as "Fields that have stable and broadly acknowledged centers, peripheries, and status orders will be more homogeneous both because the diffusion structure for new models and norms is more routine and because the level of interaction among organizations in the field is high" (DiMaggio and Powell, 1983).
3 In the cases examined, uncertainty led to Finnish auditors modelling their work on the private sector, and Norwegian auditors using the public sector as a model (Johnsen *et al.*, 2001).
4 The statements provided were: In order to ensure accountability for delegated authority/allocation of resources (agency theory); a high-quality audit will send a signal to external stakeholders such as costs of borrowing and so on (signalling); external stakeholders seek political insurance from the auditor which allows them to lay blame or recover losses (insurance); audit provides assurance to the entity's top management, especially when there is decentralisation (management control); audit (including audit committees) complements corporate governance to reduce risk (corporate governance); audit confirms unaudited announcements and increases confidence in these unaudited financial statements (confirmation).
5 Pollitt and Summa (1997) apply a classification of SAIs into four categories: court, collegiate body, independent reporting to Parliament, and within the structure of the executive government.
6 Although none of the changes were "quite as exciting as those which took place in New Zealand" (Pollitt, 2003).

References

Abdel-khalik, A. R. (1993) 'Why do private companies demand auditing? A case for organizational loss of control', *Journal of Accounting, Auditing & Finance*, 8(1), pp. 31–52. https://doi.org/10.1177/0148558X9300800103.

Baber, W. R. (1983) 'Toward understanding the role of auditing in the public sector', *Journal of Accounting and Economics*, 5(C), pp. 213–227. https://doi.org/10.1016/0165-4101(83)90013-7.

Baker, C. R., Bédard, J. and Prat dit Hauret, C. (2014) 'The regulation of statutory auditing: An institutional theory approach', *Managerial Auditing Journal*, 29(5), pp. 371–394. https://doi.org/10.1108/MAJ-09-2013-0931.

Ball, R. and Brown, P. (1968) 'An empirical evaluation of accounting income numbers', *Journal of Accounting Research*, 6(2), pp. 159–178.

Ball, R., Jayaraman, S. and Shivakumar, L. (2012) 'Audited financial reporting and voluntary disclosure as complements: A test of the confirmation hypothesis', *Journal of Accounting and Economics*. Elsevier, 53(1–2), pp. 136–166. https://doi.org/10.1016/j.jacceco.2011.11.005.

Banker, R. D., Cooper, W. W. and Potter, G. (1992) 'A perspective on research in governmental accounting', *The Accounting Review*, 67(3), pp. 496–510.

Barzelay, M. (1997) 'Central audit institutions and performance auditing: A comparative analysis of organizational strategies in the OECD', *Governance*, 10(3), pp. 235–260. https://doi.org/10.1111/0952-1895.411997041.

Basu, O., Dirsmith, M. W. and Gupta, P. P. (1999) 'The coupling of the symbolic and the technical in an institutionalized context: The negotiated order of the GAO's audit reporting process', *American Sociological Review*, 64(4), pp. 506–526.

Bédard, J. and Compernolle, T. (2014) 'The external auditor and the audit committee', in Hay, D., Knechel, W. R. and Willekens, M. (eds.), *Routledge Companion to Auditing*. Abingdon, Oxon, UK: Routledge, pp. 253–263.

Blume, L. and Voigt, S. (2011) 'Does organizational design of supreme audit institutions matter? A cross-country assessment', *European Journal of Political Economy*. Elsevier B.V., 27(2), pp. 215–229. https://doi.org/10.1016/j.ejpoleco.2010.07.001.

Bonollo, E. (2019) 'Measuring supreme audit institutions' outcomes: Current literature and future insights', *Public Money & Management*. Taylor & Francis, 39(7), pp. 468–77. https://doi.org/10.1080/09540962.2019.1583887.

Botica Redmayne, N., Bradbury, M. E. and Cahan, S. F. (2011) 'The association between audit committees and audit fees in the public sector', *International Journal of Auditing*, 15(3), pp. 301–315. https://doi.org/10.1111/j.1099-1123.2011.00436.x.

Bradbury, M. and Scott, T. (2015) 'The association between accounting performance and constituent response in political markets', *Pacific Accounting Review*, 27(4), pp. 394–410. https://doi.org/10.1108/PAR-02-2014-0007.

Broadbent, J. and Laughlin, R. (2003) 'Control and legitimation in government accountability processes: The private finance initiative in the UK', *Critical Perspectives on Accounting*, 14(1–2), pp. 23–48. https://doi.org/10.1006/cpac.2001.0525.

Carpenter, V. L. and Feroz, E. H. (2001) 'Institutional theory and accounting rule choice: An analysis of four US state governments' decisions to adopt generally accepted accounting principles', *Accounting, Organizations and Society*, 26(7–8), pp. 565–596. https://doi.org/10.1016/S0361-3682(00)00038-6.

Chan, M. X., Cordery, C. J. and van Peursem, K. (2016) 'An institutional lens on auditor-general roles in two Pacific nations: Samoa and Tonga', *Working Paper No. 107*. Centre for Accounting, Governance and Taxation Research School of Accounting and Commercial Law, Victoria, University of Wellington.

Chow, C. W. (1982) 'The demand for external auditing: Size, debt and ownership influences', *The Accounting Review*, 57(2), pp. 272–291.

Christensen, M. (2003) 'Without "reinventing the wheel": Business accounting applied to the public sector', *Australian Accounting Review*, 13(30), pp. 22–27. https://doi.org/10.1111/j.1835-2561.2003.tb00396.x.

Christensen, M. (2005) 'The "third hand": Private sector consultants in public sector accounting change', *European Accounting Review*, 14(3), pp. 447–474. https://doi.org/10.1080/0963818042000306217.

Clark, C. and De Martinis, M. (2003) 'A framework for reforming the independence and accountability of statutory Officers of Parliament: A case study of Victoria', *Australian Journal of Public Administration*, 62(1), pp. 32–42. https://doi.org/10.1111/1467-8500.00312.

Cordery, C. J. and Hay, D. (2018) 'Supreme Audit Institutions and public value: Demonstrating relevance', *Financial Accountability & Management*, 35(2), pp. 128–142.

DiMaggio, P. J. and Powell, W. W. (1983) 'The iron cage revisited: Institutional isomorphism and collective rationality in organizational fields', *American Sociological Review*, 48(2), pp. 147–160.

Elliott, R. K. (1994) 'The future of audits', *Journal of Accountancy*, 178(3), pp. 74–82.

Evans III, J. H. E. and Patton, J. M. (1987) 'Signaling and monitoring in public-sector accounting', *Journal of Accounting Research*, 25(May), p. 130. https://doi.org/10.2307/2491083.

Frumkin, P. and Galaskiewicz, J. (2004) 'Institutional isomorphism and public sector organizations', *Journal of Public Administration Research and Theory*, 14(3), pp. 283–307. https://doi.org/10.1093/jopart/muh028.

González-Díaz, B. and García-Fernández, R. (2017) 'What about supreme audit institutions? A literature review and suggestions for future research', in *40th European Accounting Aassociation Annual Congress. Valencia, 10-12 May.*

Gupta, P. P., Dirsmith, M. W. and Fogarty, T. J. (1994) 'Coordination and control in a government agency: Contingency and institutional theory perspectives on GAO audits', *Administrative Science Quarterly*, 39(2), p. 264. https://doi.org/10.2307/2393236.

Hay, D. (2001) 'Public sector decentralization, accountability and financial reporting in New Zealand', *Public Budgeting, Accounting & Financial Management*, 13(2), pp. 133–156.

Hay, D. (2003) 'Knowledge transfer costs and dependence as determinants of financial reporting', *Accounting and Finance*, 43(3), pp. 311–330. https://doi.org/10.1111/j.1467-629x.2003.00093.x.

Hay, D. and Cordery, C. J. (2018) 'The value of public sector audit: Literature and history', *Journal of Accounting Literature*. Elsevier, 40(June), pp. 1–15. https://doi.org/https://doi.org/10.1016/j.acclit.2017.11.0010737-4607/.

Heald, D. (2018) 'Transparency-generated trust: The problematic theorization of public audit', *Financial Accountability & Management*, (June), pp. 1–19. https://doi.org/10.1111/faam.12175.

Hofstede, G. (1980) *Culture's Consequences: International Differences in Work-Related Values*. Beverly Hills, CA: Sage Publications.

Hofstede, G. (2001) *Culture's Consequences: Comparing Values, Behaviors, Institutions and Organizations Across Nations*. 2nd edn. Thousand Oaks, CA: Sage Publications.

Hood, C. (1995) 'The "new public management" in the 1980s: Variations on a theme', *Accounting, Organizations and Society*, 20(2–3), pp. 93–109. https://doi.org/10.1016/0361-3682(93)E0001-W.

Jacobs, K. (2012) 'Making sense of social practice: Theoretical pluralism in public sector accounting research', *Financial Accountability & Management*, 28(1), pp. 1–25. https://doi.org/10.1111/j.1468-0408.2011.00534.x.

James, O. and John, P. (2007) 'Public management at the ballot box: Performance information and electoral support for incumbent English local governments',

Journal of Public Administration Research and Theory, 17(4), pp. 567–580. https://doi.org/10.1093/jopart/mul020.

Jensen, K. L. (2005) 'A basic study of agency-cost source and municipal use of internal versus external control', *Accounting and Business Research*, 35(1), pp. 53–67. https://doi.org/10.1080/00014788.2005.9729662.

Johnsen, Å. (2019) 'Public sector audit in contemporary society: A short review and introduction', *Financial Accountability & Management*, 35(2), pp. 121–127. https://doi.org/10.1111/faam.12191.

Johnsen, Å. *et al.* (2001) 'Performance auditing in local government: An exploratory study of perceived efficiency of municipal value for money auditing in Finland and Norway', *The European Accounting Review*, 10(3), pp. 583–599. https://doi.org/10.1080/09638180120081580.

Judge, W. *et al.* (2010) 'National adoption of international accounting standards: An institutional perspective', *Corporate Governance: An International Review*, 18(3), pp. 161–174. https://doi.org/10.1111/j.1467-8683.2010.00798.x.

Keerasuntonpong, P. and Cordery, C. J. (2018) 'How might normative and mimetic pressures improve local government service performance reporting?', *Accounting and Finance*, 58(4), pp. 1169–1200. https://doi.org/10.1111/acfi.12252.

Khan, S. H. and Hoque, Z. (2016) 'Changes in the public accounts committee of a less developed democratic country: A field study', *Financial Accountability and Management*, 32(1), pp. 80–103. https://doi.org/10.1111/faam.12082.

Lamoreaux, P. T. *et al.* (2015) 'Do accounting and audit quality affect World Bank lending?', *The Accounting Review*, 90(2), pp. 703–738. https://doi.org/10.2308/accr-50865.

La Porta *et al.* (2006) 'What works in securities laws?', *Journal of Finance*, 61(1), pp. 1–32. https://doi.org/10.1111/j.1540-6261.2006.00828.x.

Modell, S. (2013) 'Making sense of social practice: Theoretical pluralism in public sector accounting research: A comment', *Financial Accountability & Management*, 29(1), pp. 99–110. https://doi.org/10.1111/faam.12004.

Moe, T. M. (1984) 'The new economics of organization', *American Journal of Political Science*, 28(4), pp. 739–777.

Moore, M. H. (1995) *Creating Public Value: Strategic Management in Government*. Cambridge, MA: Harvard University Press.

Moore, M. H. (2013) *Recognizing Public Value*. Cambridge, MA & London: Harvard University Press.

Morin, D. (2001) 'Influence of value for money audit on Public Administrations: Looking beyond appearances', *Financial Accountability & Management*, 17(2), pp. 99–117. https://doi.org/10.1111/1468-0408.00123.

Morin, D. (2014) 'Auditors General's impact on administrations: A pan-Canadian study (2001–2011)', *Managerial Auditing Journal*, 29(5), pp. 395–426. https://doi.org/10.1108/MAJ-10-2013-0948.

Mulgan, R. (1997) 'The processes of public accountability', *Australian Journal of Public Administration*, 56(1), pp. 25–36.

Oulasvirta, L. (2014) 'The reluctance of a developed country to choose International Public Sector Accounting Standards of the IFAC. A critical case study',

Critical Perspectives on Accounting. Elsevier Ltd, 25(3), pp. 272–285. https://doi.org/10.1016/j.cpa.2012.12.001.

Pilcher, R. (2011) 'Implementing IFRS in local government: Institutional isomorphism as NPM goes mad?', *Local Government Studies*, 37(4), pp. 367–389. https://doi.org/10.1080/03003930.2011.588702.

Pollitt, C. (2003) 'Performance audit in Western Europe: Trends and choices', *Critical Perspectives on Accounting*, 14(1–2), pp. 157–170. https://doi.org/10.1006/cpac.2002.0521.

Pollitt, C. and Summa, H. (1997) 'Comparative and international administration reflexive watchdogs? How Supreme Audit institutions account for themselves', *Public Administration*, 75, pp. 313–336. https://doi.org/10.1111/1467-9299.00063.

Power, M. K. (1997) *The Audit Society: Rituals of Verification*. Oxford: Oxford University Press.

Reichborn-Kjennerud, K. *et al.* (2019) 'SAIs work against corruption in Scandinavian, South-European and African countries: An institutional analysis', *British Accounting Review*, 51(5). https://doi.org/10.1016/j.bar.2019.100842.

Sanders, G. and Allen, A. C. (1993) 'Signaling government financial reporting quality to credit analysts', *Public Budgeting & Finance*, 13(3), pp. 73–84. https://doi.org/10.1111/1540-5850.00984.

Skærbæk, P. (2009) 'Public sector auditor identities in making efficiency auditable: The National Audit Office of Denmark as independent auditor and modernizer', *Accounting, Organizations and Society*, 34(8), pp. 971–987. https://doi.org/10.1016/j.aos.2009.01.001.

Stapenhurst, R. and Titsworth, J. (2001) 'Features and functions of supreme audit institutions', *Prem Notes 59*. Washington, DC: World Bank Institute, pp. 1–4. Available at: https://openknowledge.worldbank.org/handle/10986/9766.

Streim, H. (1994) 'Agency problems in the legal political system and supreme auditing institutions', *European Journal of Law and Economics*, 1(3), pp. 177–191. https://doi.org/10.1007/BF01552469.

Titman, S. and Trueman, B. (1986) 'Information quality and the valuation of new issues', *Journal of Accounting and Economics*, 8, pp. 159–172.

Wallace, W. A. (1980) *The Economic Role of the Audit in Free and Regulated Markets*. New York NY.: Touche Ross Foundation.

Yamamoto, K. and Kim, M. J. (2019) 'Stakeholders' approach on government auditing in the supreme audit institutions of Japan and Korea', *Financial Accountability & Management*, (June 2018), pp. 1–16. https://doi.org/10.1111/faam.12187.

Zimmerman, J. L. (1977) 'The municipal accounting maze: An analysis of political incentives', *Journal of Accounting Research*, 15, p. 107. https://doi.org/10.2307/2490636.

3 Supreme Audit Institutions around the world

3.1 Introduction

SAIs are important organisations. They exist in virtually all countries and have been shown to have an impact on government accountability and management. Differences among the types of SAIs in different countries are well known. In this chapter we present an analysis of data related to the issues of what types of SAI there are and what SAI activities occur in countries around the world. We examine data on variables related to the explanations for SAI structure and activities.

The World Bank classification of SAIs into court, Westminster and board models is widely used (Stapenhurst and Titsworth, 2001), and there are other classifications. The first question we look at is, how many of each model of SAI exist? A related question is how well the SAIs fit into these models described in the literature and to what extent do they have unique features? It may be the case that countries all adopt variations in their SAI models to fit their local circumstances, so that the classifications are therefore too general to describe SAIs very well.

There are also other differences apart from the SAI model, especially how much of the public sector each SAI takes responsibility for. Some SAIs are auditors of purely the national or federal government, while others cover a wider range of public sector institutions. At the same time, SAIs can concentrate to a greater or lesser extent on compliance auditing, financial report auditing or performance auditing, and there are variations along that dimension as well.

We then look at what factors are the influences on the structure and activity of SAIs. Chapter 2 set out how three sets of influences could lead to isomorphism, where the SAIs would come to follow a model set by other institutions. The SAIs could be subject to coercive, mimetic and normative influences that might cause some degree of isomorphism. These isomorphic influences could lead to the SAIs converging on one model, but it does not necessarily have to be the case that they will all converge upon a single model. Isomorphism could result in the SAIs converging upon one of a small number of categories. Chapter 2 also discusses how other reasons why auditing exists can influence the demand for auditing and sets out six explanations for the value of auditing that are likely to be relevant. In accordance with some of these explanations, previous research has also shown that the structure of government itself has an impact on the structure of the SAI; meanwhile the structure of government institutions is itself influenced by factors such as isomorphism. In recent years, SAIs have increased the extent to which they collaborate with each other through INTOSAI and the International Congress of Supreme Audit Institutions (INCOSAI) (INTOSAI IDI Development Initiative, 2017). As a result, we may see an increasing trend to isomorphism compared to earlier studies.

The questions that we investigate are, first, what are the categories of SAI and how well do they fit the models used in the literature? Second, we examine to what extent are variables that measure the influences of isomorphism associated with the form and activities of SAIs. Third, we consider to what extent are variables for the explanations for the value of auditing associated with the form and activities of SAIs; and fourth, we examine other influences such as culture. Last, we consider the effectiveness of the different models. Chapter 2 also examined Moore's (2013) model of how public entities engage themselves in building value for society. Some SAIs report on public value. We examine the question of to what extent that relates to the model of SAI and other SAI variables in each jurisdiction.

3.2 Sources and analysis and the audit activities undertaken

Our information for analysis was drawn mainly from public sources and our survey. The public sources included publications by INTOSAI and regional SAI bodies, especially EUROSAI (European Court of Auditors, 2019); INTOSAI's database; and data from international organisations like the World Bank.

INTOSAI's database maintained by the SAI of Mexico was very useful. The database includes information about SAIs provided by a large number of SAIs. The information was gathered in 2013–2014. The Director of the INTOSAI General Secretariat, Dr Monika González-Koss and Mr Francisco T. Parral-Pineda, Departmental Chief of the National Anti-Corruption System Division of the Auditoria Superior de la Federacíon, very helpfully provided access to INTOSAI's database maintained by the SAI of Mexico. The database's webpage states that:

> The INTOSAI SAI's Information Database is aimed at gathering and making available information such as SAIs' organization, administrative characteristics, mandate, scope, and auditing practices, as well as data on their communication methods and reporting, among other topics.
>
> (INTOSAI, 2019)

The data is gathered from an information tool that SAIs can use. For many items, data is available in the database for a large number of SAIs (more than 90), but it does not include data from all INTOSAI jurisdictions. There are missing observations for many of the variables that we include. Another valuable source is the European Court of Auditors Handbook (2019) which provides an overview of the "mandate, status, organization, work and output of the 29 supreme audit institutions of the EU and its Member States and illustrate(s) the differences and similarities between them" (European Court of Auditors, 2019, p. 4).

We also used data from the World Bank, from Transparency International and from other publicly available sources. Our own survey also provides specific information about SAI activities.

All of our sources have limitations, especially that they do not provide complete information. They can also be inconsistent since different SAIs may have differing interpretations of the terms that are used in different datasets. Nevertheless, the sources provide information that is helpful and are the most comprehensive sources available.

3.3 SAI models and their activities

3.3.1 SAI models

According to the published literature, SAIs tend to follow one of three or four types. In the World Bank classification, there are three models: court (or Napoleonic or judicial), Westminster and board (Stapenhurst and Titsworth, 2001, p. 1). There are four main types according to a classification used by Pollitt and Summa (1997) – the court with judicial functions, the collegiate body, the independent audit office reporting to a Parliament and the audit office within the structure of executive government. Pollitt and Summa (1997) regard the Swedish and Finnish SAIs as being within the structure of government. Bonollo (2019, p. 4) also uses the four models and observes that the Swedish SAI was no longer part of government after 2003.

The OECD uses the three-model (World Bank) classification (OECD, 2012). The INTOSAI database collected information from SAIs and allowed them to use five possible models. These are Westminster; board/collegial; court/judicial; part of a Ministry of Finance; and other institutional model. These represent the four-type model, plus a recognition that some SAIs may not fit the standard models. We found that many SAIs classify themselves under more than one model category.

Reviewing the data available shows that all of these classifications are something of a convenient simplification. The data in Tables 3.1 and 3.2 show types of SAIs. These are drawn from the INTOSAI database in Table 3.1 and from the handbook by the European Court of Auditors (2019) in Table 3.2.

There are evidently a number of unique features of SAIs. Many countries report having more than one type of SAI function; for example, Belgium and five other countries report having a model that is both board/collegial and court/judicial. Some have a unique feature of their own; for example, Sweden has three auditor-generals. There are other unique features within many SAIs (for example, Vietnam – 'Court/Judicial Model, Part of Ministry

Table 3.1 SAI models according to the INTOSAI database

Type	*Number*	*Comments*
Board/collegial model	22	Frequently Asia or Europe
Court/judicial model	5	El Salvador, France, New Caledonia, Timor-Leste, Togo
Westminster model	50	The majority of jurisdictions
Other institutional model	6	India, Micronesia, Nauru, Northern Mariana Islands, Rwanda, Switzerland
Board/collegial model and Court/judicial model	6	Belgium, Brazil, Mauritania, Portugal, Spain, Turkey
Board/collegial model and Other institutional model	1	Sierra Leone
Court/judicial model, Part of Ministry of Finance and Other institutional model	1	Vietnam
Westminster and Court/judicial model	1	Chile
Westminster and Other institutional model	2	Guatemala, Kuwait
Information not provided	122	
Total	216	

Table 3.2 SAI models in the European Union (European Court of Auditors, 2019)

Type	*Number*	*Countries*
Audit office independent of government headed by an auditor-general (or president)	13	Bulgaria, Croatia, Cyprus, Denmark, Estonia, Finland, Hungary, Ireland, Lithuania, Malta, Poland, Sweden,[1] United Kingdom
Westminster	2	Austria, Slovakia
Court of audit	6	Belgium, France, Greece, Italy, Portugal, Spain
Collegiate structure with no jurisdictional function	6	Czech Republic, Germany, Latvia, Luxembourg, Netherlands, Romania
Distinct model, headed by a president and auditing at central, regional and local levels with no jurisdictional powers	1	Slovenia
Total	28	

[1] Sweden has three auditor-generals.

of Finance and Other Institutional Model'). It is also notable how many missing observations there are in the INTOSAI database, so that there may be other types as yet not described in the literature. Nevertheless, there are some distinct types, and these tend to coincide with the previous research. The most widely used model is the Westminster model, often called something like "audit office independent of government headed by an Auditor-General".[1] The court model is used widely, mostly in Francophone or Latin American countries. The board model is used in Germany and some neighbouring countries, and in a few other countries around the world.

The data shows that while SAIs have similarities, and there is some evidence of isomorphism, in which SAIs are moving towards a standard model, the extent of similarity should not be overstated. Each country is likely to have some unique features. It is also very clear that there is as yet no single standard model. Neo-institutional theory and isomorphism appear to have limitations in their application to the field of SAIs, at least so far. Nevertheless, similar isomorphic forces could be encouraging SAIs to converge on one of the three major models that exist around the world; and there may ultimately be greater convergence towards one of the models. At present, the Westminster model appears to be the most widely used, although each country also has its unique features.

Tables 3.1 and 3.2 also report inconsistent information from each other. For example, the European Court of Auditors data shows much more use of the court model than the INTOSAI data does, and some countries, for example Spain, are classified differently in one table compared to the other. As noted, the INTOSAI database also shows that many countries choose more than one classification. The inconsistencies highlight the limitations of the models as descriptions of the type of auditing practised in each country. Previous research also demonstrates the uncertainty of classifying SAIs; for example, Blume and Voigt (2011) classified a number of countries as using the court model when those countries currently appear to regard themselves as using a different model.[2]

From this analysis, we conclude that the three-model classification (Westminster, court and board) is still useful. The category 'audit office within the structure of executive government' is no longer widely used. However, there are many unique features, and many SAIs combine several models.

3.3.2 Activities

The activities of the SAIs also vary widely from bodies that concentrate on national level auditing to those that cover a wider range of institutions. Table 3.3 and Table 3.4 examine these activities for the worldwide data and for Europe respectively. Table 3.3 shows that most commonly, SAIs have a broad coverage of the entire public sector, including local government as well as the national level, and including what the database describes as 'public companies' (state-owned enterprises).

Table 3.4 examines the scope and extent of auditing in Europe. We have added a calculation of the SAI budget per unit of population and the Blume and Voigt (2011) measure of financial independence (number of SAI employees per 100,000 inhabitants). The budget per unit of population figures shows substantial variation, from as low as 1.14 Euros per 100,000 population for the UK to 7.62 for Luxembourg. The comparison suggests that the size of the country is important and that there appear to be fixed costs in establishing and running an SAI that are larger per head of population in a small country. Table 3.4 also shows that, nevertheless, both large countries and small countries can vary a lot. For example, Italy has high expenditure per head (5.13) compared to Spain (1.33), or Malta (7.39) compared to the Slovak Republic (1.97), despite their similar populations. The figures on 'percentage of state budget' do not seem to be comparable with each other, and SAIs may have used differing denominators in their calculations. Whether or not local government is part of the SAI's function is also shown in the table. This difference does not appear to have an impact on SAI budget in a country. This result could be because these costs are recovered by the SAI from the local governments concerned. We observed that as well as local government, there are other variations regarding whether SAIs audit

Table 3.3 The scope of audit according to the INTOSAI database

Scope of audit	*Number of jurisdictions*	*Number of audits conducted during the year*	*Mean number of audits conducted during the year*
Federal or national level	9	5,292	588
Federal or national level, Regional level, Local or municipal level	3	187	62
Federal or national level, Regional level, Local or municipal level, Public companies/other agencies	40	69,340	1,734
Federal or national level, Regional level, Public companies/other agencies	6	1,427	238
Federal or national level, Local or municipal level	1	112	112
Federal or national level, Local or municipal level, Public companies/other agencies	18	22,603	1,256
Federal or national level, Public companies/other agencies	14	2,398	171
Regional level, Local or municipal level, Public companies/other agencies	1	14	14
Local or municipal level, Public companies/other agencies	1	161	161
Local or municipal level	1	NA	–
Not indicated	4	65	65
Not available	131	NA	–
Grand total	229	101,599	1,224

NA: Not available

Mean of the grand total excludes countries for which number of audits is not stated.

regional government or publicly owned companies. Some SAIs are also responsible for the audit of churches (e.g. Hungary) and some for audits of political parties (e.g. Croatia).

Regarding the question of isomorphism and of whether a particular type of SAI is more efficient, we summarised large and small countries within Europe in Table 3.5. There is a tendency for larger countries to use the collegial or court type of SAI and for small countries to use the Westminster model. The table also shows the mean audit expenditure per 100,000 people

Table 3.4 The scope and extent of auditing in Europe

Jurisdiction	*SAI budget in Euros*	*Euros per 100k people*	*Independ-ence*[1]	*Percentage of state budget*	*Type of SAI*	*Local government included*
Austria	33,500,000	3.80	4.05	0.04%	Westminster/independent of Parliament	Yes
Belgium	49,400,000	4.33		0.01%	Court	No
Bulgaria	8,300,000	1.17		0.15%	Westminster/independent of Parliament	Yes
Croatia	7,600,000	1.83		0.03%	Westminster/independent of Parliament	Yes
Cyprus	5,500,000	6.50	14.31	0.07%	Westminster/independent of Parliament	Yes
Czech Republic	71,300,000	6.72		0.04%	Collegiate	No
Denmark	30,000,000	5.19	5.15	<0.01%	Westminster/independent of Parliament	No
Estonia	6,000,000	4.55		0.05%	Westminster/independent of Parliament	Yes
Finland	16,000,000	2.90	1.74	0.30%	Westminster/independent of Parliament	No
France	214,000,000	3.19	1.59	<0.01%	Court	Yes
Germany	149,000,000	1.80	0.85	0.04%	Collegiate	No
Greece	33,200,000	3.08	8.36	<0.01%	Court	Yes
Hungary	29,800,000	3.05	3.33	<0.05%	Westminster/independent of Parliament	Yes
Ireland	14,000,000	2.84	3.55	<0.02%	Westminster/independent of Parliament	No
Italy	310,000,000	5.13		<0.01%	Court	Yes
Latvia	6,200,000	3.21		0.07%	Westminster/independent of Parliament	Yes
Lithuania	9,200,000	3.28		<.05%	Westminster/independent of Parliament	Yes
Luxembourg	4,500,000	7.62		Not stated	Collegiate	No
Malta	3,400,000	7.39		0.10%	Westminster/independent of Parliament	Yes
Netherlands	28,600,000	1.66	2.14	0.11%	Collegiate	No

Poland	67,000,000	1.74	3.76	0.07%	Collegiate	Yes
Portugal	26,100,000	2.53		<0.01%	Collegiate court	Yes
Romania	58,000,000	2.95	0.11	0.17%	Collegiate	Yes
Slovak Republic	10,700,000	1.97		0.07%	Westminster-type (monocratic) structure with no jurisdictional function	Yes
Slovenia	5,600,000	2.71		0.92%	Distinct model, headed by a president and auditing at central, regional and local levels with no jurisdictional powers	Yes
Spain	62,000,000	1.33	1.53	0.01%	Court	Yes
Sweden	36,600,000	3.61	5.69	0.15%	Westminster/independent of Parliament	No
United Kingdom	75,000,000	1.14	1.41	Not stated	Westminster/independent of Parliament	No
Total	1,370,500,000					

[1] FIND measure (Blume and Voigt, 2011).

for the countries included in each group. There are no substantial differences in expenditure among the different models.

The types of audits conducted by SAIs are most usually compliance audits, financial audits and performance audits.[3] Table 3.6 shows to what

Table 3.5 Mean audit expenditure in Europe by country and number of observations broken down by SAI model and size (greater or smaller than 10 million population)

SAI model	*Mean audit expenditure in Euros per 100,000 population (number of obs. in parentheses)*	
	Large countries	*Small countries*
Westminster	2.38 (2)	3.67 (13)
Court	3.41 (5)	– (0)
Collegial	2.90 (6)	7.62 (1)

Westminster: Includes 'Audit office independent of government'.
(Excludes Slovenia, which describes itself as having a 'distinct model').

Table 3.6 Types of audits conducted

Types of audit	*Number of SAIs*	*Countries*	*Comments*
Financial audits Compliance audits Performance audits	80	All other respondents	
Financial audits Compliance audits	9	Eritrea Mexico Nauru Panama Puerto Rico Saudi Arabia Slovenia Timor-Leste Uruguay	Geographically and culturally diverse countries that are not well known in public sector auditing research
Financial audits Performance audits	4	Canada New Zealand Sweden United Kingdom	Countries using the Westminster system and perceived as innovative among SAIs
Compliance audits Performance audits	1	Brazil	
No response	134	Includes Italy, Spain, Russia, US, among many others	A limitation of the data

extent each category is conducted. Most of the SAIs that provided information to the INTOSAI database state that they carry out all three. There is a group of countries having similar audit structures and to some extent similar culture that does not report that they carry out compliance audits (Canada, New Zealand, Sweden and the United Kingdom). These countries are often seen as leaders in public sector auditing. Another nine, very diverse, countries do not include performance audits. This limited data suggest that countries with more advanced public sector auditing are more likely to conduct performance audits and less likely to conduct compliance audits.

The more comprehensive data available for the European Union (European Court of Auditors, 2019) show a similar pattern. There are nine countries reporting that they carry out financial and performance auditing[4] (Austria, Belgium, the Czech Republic, Denmark, Luxembourg, the Netherlands, Poland, Sweden and the UK). Most others report that they carry out all three types. Quite a number add other types of audit, such as environmental or IT audit. Two have unique descriptions: Greece, "ex ante, precontractual and ex post plus targeted audits (which may be financial, performance or compliance)"[5] and France, "methods defined by the court according to international standards".

We conclude from the analysis of SAI activities that most SAIs conduct all three types of audits. There are some that do not conduct compliance audits and a few that do not conduct performance audits.

3.3.3 Further supporting information from our survey

As we discussed in Chapters 1 and 2, the data was supplemented by our survey of SAIs. The survey was answered by SAIs which were geographically diverse and, across the sample, used all the different forms that are described in this chapter. Sixty percent of the SAIs were mainly funded from the state budget with funds independently set by Parliament. The balance of our sample has their budgets set by a ministry under control of the executive government. None of the SAIs received their prime funding from charging audit fees to auditees. As to the mandate of our survey sample, this was also varied. As can be seen by Figure 3.1, a great majority of SAIs in the sample undertake audits of government departments, ministries, local authorities (including provinces/regions) and the whole of government. Just over a quarter (27%) also have a mandate to audit state-owned enterprises.

Ten percent of the SAI respondents have a mandate to audit 'all entities that receive public money' or similar.[6] A small number qualified the notion of auditing state-owned enterprises as those which had more than 50% (or 51%) of public ownership.

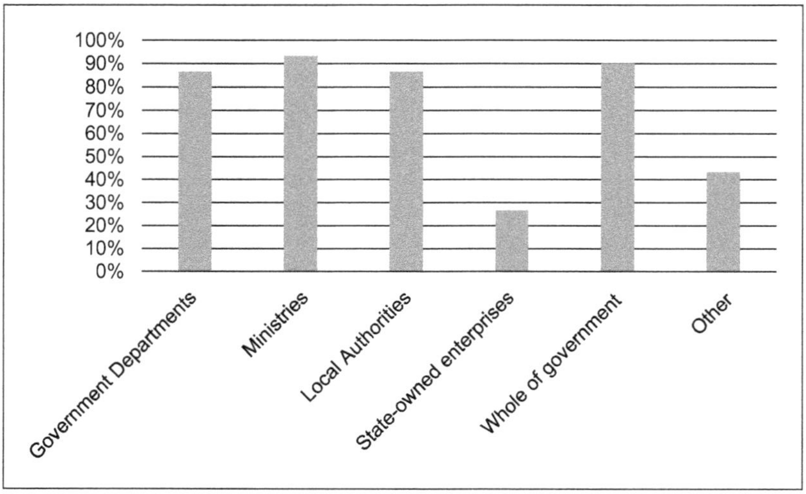

Figure 3.1 Mandate of surveyed SAIs

The SAI survey respondents also provided information on the types of audit standards that they use, with approximately half of them using International Standards of Audit either entirely or as a base to be adopted and the other half using INTOSAI standards (International Standards of Supreme Audit Institutions – ISSAIs), with some augmentations and adaptations.

The activity of these surveyed SAIs also varied widely, with the percentage of total work, as measured by the number of audits for the sample, being shown in Table 3.7.

SAIs also noted that they undertook other work, such as research and development, jurisdictional audits of accounts, investigation of indications of irregular facts/special audits and investigations, evaluations of public policies and IT audits.

When asked what percentage of their expenditure was related to these different audits, the surveyed SAIs responded as shown in Table 3.8.

It was noted that expenditure was also required on the other activities noted here, as well as support of global operations such as INTOSAI and the regional bodies of INTOSAI/the International Development Corporation. It should of course be noted that the percentages reported are approximations and would fluctuate from year to year, but they do provide an understanding of the variety of the SAIs who responded to the survey.

Table 3.7 Percentage of total work of surveyed SAIs (as measured by the number of audits)

	Minimum	*Maximum*	*Mean*	*Std Dev.*
Compliance audit (per ISSAI 400)	0.00	100.00	16.32	28.15
Financial statement audit	0.00	90.00	22.17	31.24
Performance audit	0.00	80.00	10.50	20.32

Table 3.8 Percentage of total expenditure of surveyed SAIs on main activities

	Minimum	*Maximum*	*Mean*	*Std Dev.*
Compliance audit (per ISSAI 400)	0.00	100.00	13.70	26.51
Financial statement audit	0.00	90.00	13.00	24.00
Performance audit	0.00	70.00	6.03	13.55

3.4 Isomorphism

We now turn to the issue of factors that influence isomorphism among SAIs. DiMaggio and Powell (1983) suggest that these can be categorised as coercive (dependence on other organisations), mimetic (copying other organisations because of uncertainty) and normative (following the lead of other professional people). The previous research that applied neo-institutional theory to differences in accounting standards among countries (Judge *et al.*, 2010) used foreign aid as a measure of the extent of coercive isomorphism, import penetration (representing openness to outside influences) for mimetic isomorphism and education level for normative isomorphism. A study of private sector auditing standards implies that capital markets can be a coercive influence (Baker *et al.*, 2014). In our examination of the three types of isomorphism, we have considered those measures and developed others where appropriate that are consistent with the DiMaggio and Powell model. These variables are displayed in a number of tables throughout the chapter.

3.4.1 *Coercive isomorphism*

Measures of coercive isomorphic influences can include the extent of government debt (Lamoreaux *et al.*, 2015) and foreign aid (Judge *et al.*, 2010). Measures of aid might be inaccurate, and so GDP per head might also be relevant because countries with a lower GDP are more likely to receive aid. We obtained these measures from the World Bank database. The study by Baker *et al.* (2014) suggests that capital markets may influence isomorphism, so far as auditing of listed companies is concerned, and it may be that this influence also spreads to the public sector within a country. We included total market capitalisation of the stock market in each jurisdiction, using World Bank data, as a measure of the extent to which coercive isomorphism from a need for financial markets to comply with global norms could be important.

As noted, a substantially larger number of countries use the Westminster model compared to the numbers using the other models. Westminster appears to be becoming the standard model, and if there are isomorphic pressures, they are more likely to be driving SAIs towards that model.

Table 3.9 reports information about the SAI model from the INTOSAI database and statistical measures for coercive isomorphic influences from World Bank data. The results are not entirely as expected. Countries receiving the most aid are those using the court/judicial model, but the amount of aid that they receive is only slightly more than that received by countries using the Westminster model. The board/collegial countries include developed countries such as Germany, Japan and the United Arab Emirates, and which have low average levels of foreign aid and high GDP per head. The court/judicial countries include low-income and high-aid countries like

Table 3.9 Coercive isomorphism: SAI model and mean of coercive influences

SAI model	*Count of model*	*Aid (ODA)*	*GDP per head*	*Debt, millions*	*Market capitalisation millions*
Board/collegial	22	0.961	21,827	338,674	525,056
Board/collegial and Court/judicial	6	1.033	19,011	189,485	362,134
Board/collegial and Other institutional model	1	14.811	489	1,712	–
Court/judicial	5	3.622	9,011	3,880	473,190
Court/judicial and Part of Ministry of Finance and Other institutional model	1	1.116	2,342	108,096	132,652
Other institutional model	6	9.448	20,397	396,923	587,440
Westminster	50	3.373	16,873	86,794	96,775
Westminster and Court/judicial model	1	0.026	14,830	186,697	250,739
Westminster and Other institutional model	2	0.247	16,640	11,174	–
Grand total/Mean	94	3.056	17,628	166,460	264,221

Source: Model from INTOSAI database; statistical information from World Bank.

Timor-Leste and Togo, and Mauritania (which uses a mixed board/collegial and court judicial model). The countries using the Westminster model have aid levels almost as high as the court/judicial countries, although their income is higher. The Westminster grouping includes a wide degree of variation, with many high-income countries (e.g. Iceland and New Zealand) that do not receive aid as well as very low-income countries (Ethiopia and South Sudan) that receive high levels of aid.

Debt is included as a measure of coercive isomorphism because it has been used in previous studies and because lending organisations are likely to have some influence on auditing (if they decide to use it). However, the countries with high levels of debt are usually large, advanced economies, and these countries also tend to have high incomes, which is why the board/collegial model countries have the highest debt. The Westminster model countries again also have a high degree of variation. Data is missing from the statistics for some wealthier countries, in addition.

It seemed plausible that countries with high stock market capitalisation would be influenced by investors and financial market participants to adopt similar institutions to countries with large and important stock markets. These countries include the United States, United Kingdom and others following a similar Anglo-American model. It is therefore expected that if this influence is important, these countries would adopt the Westminster model, which can be seen as an Anglo-American approach to auditing. That is not what we found. The countries using other models apart from the Westminster model all have approximately similar average market capitalisation, while market capitalisation for the Westminster countries is much smaller. This result is influenced by a large number of countries in the Westminster group which the World Bank reports as having no stock market.

If coercive isomorphism is relevant, then more aid or lower national income, higher debt or greater share of market capitalisation will be associated with the Westminster model. Our results show that is not the case. We are aware that there is some anecdotal evidence showing that these influences are important, but nevertheless, the data does not show their effect. The results in Table 3.9 show that coercive isomorphism does not appear to be a strong influence over the model adopted by SAIs. If it is, then controlling for some other factors must also be important.

3.4.2 Mimetic isomorphism

Mimetic isomorphism occurs when organisations copy their organisational form from others which are seen as successful or legitimate. According to DiMaggio and Powell (1983), organisations are more likely to imitate others when they face uncertainty. We used a broad range of measures for the level of uncertainty. Tables 3.10 to Table 3.13 show the results of examining forces for mimetic isomorphism.

We include a political stability index measure obtained from TheGlobalEconomy.com (TheGlobalEconomy.com, 2019). The measure is the

Table 3.10 Mimetic isomorphism: SAI model, political stability, political rights and civil liberties

SAI model	*No. obs.*	*Mean political stability*	*Mean political rights*	*Mean civil liberties*
Board/collegial	22	75.15	2.45	2.30
Board/collegial and Court/judicial	6	103.83	2.33	2.17
Board/collegial and Other institutional model	1	101.00	3.00	3.00
Court/judicial	5	118.67	2.75	3.25
Court/judicial and Part of Ministry of Finance and Other institutional model	1	74.00	7.00	5.00
Other institutional model	6	70.75	2.20	2.20
Westminster	50	85.45	2.52	2.50
Westminster and Court/judicial model	1	72.00	1.00	1.00
Westminster and Other institutional model	2	122.50	3.50	4.00
Not available	141	110.90	4.07	3.77
Grand total/Mean	**235**	**100.45**	**3.44**	**3.25**

Political stability ranks from 1 (most stable) to 195; political rights and civil liberties on a scale from 1 (most free) to 7.

Table 3.11 SAI model and World Bank measure of property rights and rule-based governance

SAI model	*Number*	*Mean property rights and governance*
Board/collegial	3	3.50
Board/collegial and Court/judicial	1	3.00
Board/collegial and Other institutional model	1	3.00
Court/judicial	2	2.50
Other institutional model	3	3.33
Westminster	15	2.93
Grand total/Mean	**25**	**3.02**

Table 3.12 SAI model and La Porta et al. measure of securities law enforcement

SAI model	*No. obs.*	*Mean securities law enforcement*
Board/collegial	8	0.47
Board/collegial and Court/judicial	5	0.45
Court/judicial	1	0.77
Other institutional model	2	0.50
Westminster	16	0.54
Westminster and Court/judicial model	1	0.60
Grand total/Mean	33	0.52

Table 3.13 Legal system of countries and SAI model

Jurisdiction	*English*	*French*	*German*	*Scandinavian*	*Grand total*
Board/collegial	2	7	3	–	12
Board/collegial and Court/judicial	–	6	–	–	6
Board/collegial and Other institutional model	1	–	–	–	1
Court/judicial	–	5	–	–	5
Court/judicial and Part of Ministry of Finance and Other institutional model	–	1	–	–	1
Other institutional model	3	1	1	–	5
Westminster	20	12	1	4	37
Westminster and Court/judicial model	–	1	–	–	1
Westminster and Other institutional model	1	1	–	–	2
Not available	37	47	–	1	85
Grand total	64	81	5	5	155

'Index of Political Stability and Absence of Violence/Terrorism'. It measures perceptions of the likelihood that the government will be destabilised or overthrown by unconstitutional or violent means, including politically motivated violence and terrorism. The index is a composite measure based on sources including the Economist Intelligence Unit, the World Economic Forum and the Political Risk Services, among others. It is intended to reflect how likely it is that there will be a disorderly transfer of government power, armed conflict, violent demonstrations, social unrest, international tensions and terrorism, as well as ethnic, religious or regional conflicts. The index values that we have used are the rankings from 1 and 2 as most stable (Monaco and New Zealand) to 194 and 195 (Afghanistan and Yemen).

A further measure, also included in the review of rule of law studies (Skaaning, 2010), is the Freedom House rankings of political rights and civil liberties (Puddington and Dunham, 2017). Freedom House provides country rankings for political rights and civil liberties ranging from 1 to 7, with 1 representing the most free and 7 the least free. The data is available from the website (Freedom House, 2018).

In Table 3.10, we show SAI structure together with the political stability measure (ranking from the 'Index of Political Stability and Absence of Violence/Terrorism'), and the scores for political rights and civil liberties as measures of uncertainty. The court/judicial model shows higher (less stable) mean scores than the board/collegial model or the Westminster model. When we examined the data more closely, we also saw that the Westminster model includes countries with a much wider range of scores, including stable countries with low ranks such as New Zealand and Iceland, as well as more unstable countries including Ethiopia and Venezuela. The other SAI categories do not include such extreme observations. This is consistent with the proposition that the Westminster model exists in stable countries and is the most widely used, and so it is emulated by those that are less stable, in a process of mimetic isomorphism. The results for mean political stability and mean political rights show a similar pattern, with the court/judicial jurisdictions showing higher average scores, representing reduced political rights and civil liberties. The results for jurisdictions that did not provide data to the INTOSAI database also have lower average levels of stability, rights and liberties compared to those for which information is available.

An alternative measure is the rule of law in a country. There are a number of alternatives available (Skaaning, 2010), of which the World Bank measure of CPIA property rights and rule-based governance rating is regularly updated. However, it reports data only for the poorest countries (CPIA countries, for Country Policy and Institutional Assessment, also known as countries eligible for IDA finance, from the International Development Association). These are mainly less developed countries. For this measure, higher scores indicate stronger rule of law, on a scale from 1 to 6. To cover a different range of countries, we also use a relevant business law measure, the index of securities law enforcement from La Porta *et al.* (2006, pp. 15–16), supplemented by further data added in a website supporting a later paper (Djankov *et al.*, 2008).[7] These scores are on a scale from 0 to 1, again with a higher score representing greater rule of law.

More relevant measures are the rule of law measures, but these cover a much more limited range of countries. The World Bank data cover mainly less developed countries, and we report their results in Table 3.11. These countries predominantly use the Westminster model, which in this case has a relatively low average score for property rights (representing a lower level of rule of law). This result is consistent with mimetic isomorphism whereby the countries that face greater uncertainty follow the most widely used model.

In Table 3.12, we report the results for those countries for which the La Porta measure of securities law enforcement is available. For this group, the Westminster model has the highest score (except for the one country, France, in the court/judicial category for which data is available). A higher score represents greater rule of law.

The results of Tables 3.11 and 3.12 taken together are consistent with the Westminster model being used in developing country jurisdictions that are less stable and in developed countries that are more stable.

Heald (2018, p. 1) observes that newly established countries have tended to copy the institutional arrangements of former colonial powers. He notes that "whereas these models are seen as key elements of democratic governance in the former colonial powers, the terminology has continued in countries with weak claims to be regarded as democracies". He describes this process as mimetic isomorphism, although he criticises it as being "without recognition of context". The history of countries, and in particular whether they were ruled by a colonial power, is a potential source of isomorphism. To take account of this, we include each country's legal system as an indication of its colonial history, using the classification scheme (from La Porta *et al*., 2006) that divides countries into English, French, German and Scandinavian legal systems.

We proxy those historical factors by using the legal system of a country. Table 3.13 shows the results. There is a fairly consistent pattern; since the Scandinavian countries all use a version of the Westminster system, most countries using a German-based legal system use a board/collegial system. While it might be expected that countries with a French legal system would use the court/judicial system, there are larger numbers using the Westminster and board/collegial system. Most countries using an English law-based system use a Westminster system, but there are exceptions. The idea that countries adopt a system based on their former colonising power as an outcome of mimetic isomorphism is not as widely supported as might be expected.

There is evidence, overall, that mimetic isomorphism plays a part in the SAI model in use by countries. It applies particularly to less developed countries, which might be subject to greater uncertainty. In those circumstances, these jurisdictions appear to adopt a Westminster model. The data is somewhat mixed, although some trends are clear. Countries with less political stability, fewer political rights and fewer civil liberties tend to use the court model of SAI. The Westminster model exists in a wide range of countries at more extreme ends of the scales of political stability, political rights and civil liberties, which is consistent with the less stable countries with fewer rights emulating the more stable countries with more rights, mimetically. A similar pattern applies to property rights and securities law enforcement. On the other hand, colonial history is not as strongly associated with mimetic isomorphism.

3.4.3 Normative isomorphism

Normative isomorphism is influenced by professionalisation, whereby organisations become similar to others because the managers participate in trade or professional organisations. In a previous study of accounting standards (Judge *et al.*, 2010), the education level of the population generally was used as a proxy for normative isomorphism. We examine measures of education and more specific accounting and auditing measures.

There are several professional organisations that influence SAI managers, particularly INTOSAI and the regional SAI bodies, and also professional accounting institutes that operate internationally. In countries with a strong accounting profession, covering either the public sector or the private sector (or both), these are likely to encourage an SAI to be similar to the auditing models used by the accounting profession.

A relevant measure for the strength of the accounting profession is the index created by Brown *et al.* (2014) of accounting standards. They report two measures, called auditing and enforcement, designed to capture differences between countries in relation to the auditing of financial statements and the enforcement of compliance with each country's accounting standards (Brown *et al.*, 2014, p. 1). The two measures cover "the quality of the public company auditors' working environment and the degree of accounting enforcement activity by independent enforcement bodies" for 51 countries. The auditing index includes measures for licensing, quality assurance, audit fees and litigation risk, collected from the International Federation of Accountants. The enforcement index measures the powers and activities of the body that regulates auditors. These measures are directed at private sector auditing but give a reliable measure of the quality and professionalism of the audit profession in general for each country. As such they provide a measure of potential normative influences from professional auditors. We use the 2008 index measures, which are the most recent.

An alternative, simple measure of an advanced accounting profession in a country is the use of International Financial Reporting Standards. The website www.iasplus.com maintained by Deloitte includes a list of each country's situation regarding IFRS (Deloitte, 2019). The information shown reports countries as 'IFRS not permitted', 'IFRS permitted', 'IFRS required by some firms', 'IFRS required for all firms', 'Audit report states compliance with IFRS' and 'Use of IFRSs by Unlisted Companies'. We extract from this information which countries have IFRS not permitted and for which countries IFRS is required for all. This measure indicates a country that has an advanced private sector accounting profession, which is likely to be normative influence on public sector accounting.

As a further influence, an SAI that is looking for guidance on professionalisation is very likely to seek it from its peers in regional SAI bodies such as PASAI or EUROSAI. This type of isomorphism is very plausible, as SAIs in a region cooperate with each other, hold conferences and provide many opportunities for SAIs to share ideas.

Our analysis therefore looks at the auditing and enforcement indexes from Brown *et al.* (2014) and IFRS measures, of whether IFRS is not allowed, and whether IFRS is required for at least some entities, from IAS Plus (Deloitte, 2019). We then include education overall, measured by the percentage of the population who have completed primary education and the percentage of the population with bachelor's degrees. We also examine to which regional SAI each jurisdiction belongs, obtained from the regional SAIs' websites.

Table 3.14 shows the results for auditing and accounting measures from Brown *et al.*'s (2014) index and from IAS Plus. Higher scores in the Brown index measures represent stronger auditing requirements or stronger enforcement. Higher averages, where there are more than one or two observations, appear to be associated with the Westminster model countries, and lower scores with the board/collegial countries. Similarly, a higher proportion of the Westminster countries have IFRS accounting standards required for at least some entities. There is evidence of normative isomorphism taking place, where countries with a strong auditing profession are more likely to apply the Westminster system, although the evidence is admittedly mixed.

However, the model of SAI is not something that can be easily changed, so that it might take some time for isomorphism to take effect. Table 3.15 considers the types of audits conducted by SAIs and their country's accounting and auditing requirements. This function can change more readily. The table shows that although most jurisdictions conduct all three types, there is a tendency for countries with stronger accounting requirements to be more likely to conduct performance audits and less likely to conduct compliance audits.

Table 3.16 shows the SAI models used in the jurisdictions within each regional SAI. This table illustrates the extent to which normative isomorphism takes the form of SAIs converging on the model used by other

Table 3.14 Normative isomorphism: accounting and auditing requirements and SAI model

SAI model	*No. of obs. for Brown indexes*	*Mean of audit index (Brown)*	*Mean of enforcement (Brown)*	*No. of obs. for IFRS measures*	*IFRS not allowed*	*IFRS required in some cases*
Board/collegial	10	18.90	10.80	20	3	13
Board/collegial and Court/judicial	5	22.60	13.40	5	0	3
Board/collegial and Other institutional model	–	–	–	1	0	1
Court/judicial	1	45.00	16.00	3	1	1
Court/judicial and Part of Ministry of Finance and Other institutional model			–	1	1	0
Other institutional model	2	21.00	14.00	2	0	0
Westminster	12	26.33	15.83	37	1	31
Westminster and Court/judicial Model	1	4.00	5.00	1	0	1
Westminster and Other institutional model	–	–	–	1	0	1
Not available in INTOSAI database	26	20.38	12.04	89	14	49
Grand total	57	21.74	12.75	160	20	100

Table 3.15 Normative isomorphism: accounting and auditing requirements and types of audits conducted

Types of audits	*No. obs. for Brown et al. indexes*	*Mean audit index (Brown)*	*Mean enforcement (Brown)*	*No. of obs. for IFRS measures*	*No of jurisdictions where IFRS not permitted*	*No of jurisdictions where IFRS required for some entities*
Financial audits/Compliance audits	2	11.50	10.50	4	1	3
Financial audits/Compliance audits/Performance audits	25	23.08	12.88	63	5	44
Financial audits/Performance audits	4	28.25	18.00	4	0	4
Compliance audits/Performance audits	1	15.00	8.00	1	0	1
Not available	25	20.44	12.16	88	14	48
Grand total/Mean	57	21.74	12.75	160	20	100

Table 3.16 SAI models in each regional SAI

SAI model	*AFROSAI-E*	*ARABOSAI*	*ASOSAI*	*CAROSAI*	*CREFIAF*	*EUROSAI*	*OLACEFS*	*PASAI*	*None*	*Grand total*
Board/collegial	1	1	8	1	–	7	2	2	–	22
Board/collegial and Court/judicial	–	1	–	–	–	4	1	–	–	6
Board/collegial and Other institutional model	1	–	–	–	–	–	–	–	–	1
Court/judicial	–	–	1	–	1	1	1	1	–	5
Court/judicial and Part of Ministry of Finance and Other institutional model			1	–	–	–	–	–	–	1
Other institutional model	1	–	1	–	–	1	–	3	–	6
Westminster	9	1	5	2	–	16	12	4	1	50
Westminster and Court/judicial model	–	–	–	–	–	–	1	–	–	1
Westminster and Other institutional model	–	–	1	–	–	–	1	–	–	2
Not available	14	20	31	19	19	19	4	9	6	141
Grand total	26	23	48	22	20	48	22	19	7	235

AFROSAI-E: African Organisation of English-Speaking Supreme Audit Institutions
ARABOSAI: Arab Organisation for Supreme Audit Institutions
ASOSAI: Asian Organisation of Supreme Audit Institutions
CAROSAI: Caribbean Organisation of Supreme Audit Institutions
CREFIAF: Le Conseil Régional de Formation des Institutions Supérieures de Contrôle des Finances Publiques de l'Afrique Francophone sub-Saharienne
EUROSAI: European Organisation of Supreme Audit Institutions
OLACEFS: Organización Latinoamericana y del Caribe de Entidades Fiscalizadoras Superiores
PASAI: Pacific Association of Supreme Audit Institutions

Data obtained from the regional SAI websites:
https://afrosai-e.org.za/members-contact/
www.arabosai.org/En/sai-s-members_108_208
www.asosai.org/asosai/client/web120/subject/n1/n120/n1300/n1474/index.jsp
https://carosai.org/
www.crefiaf.org/#
www.eurosai.org/en/about-us/members/
www.olacefs.com
www.pasai.org/members-map

members of the same regional SAI. Of the SAIs for which data is available, the Westminster model is most common in almost all regions, the only exception being ASOSAI (Asia) which has more entities using the board/collegial model. There is some evidence that some regions are converging on one model; for example, the Westminster model is extensively used in the OLACEFS (Latin American) region. In this case the jurisdictions for which data is not available are a substantial limitation, especially in the CREFIAF (Francophone African) and CAROSAI (Caribbean) regional groups.

We also conducted a similar analysis of the type of audit conducted in the jurisdictions within each regional SAI. The results (not reported here) do not show any apparent pattern of isomorphism within regions.

The level of education in a country is also likely to be a source of normative isomorphism. Judge *et al.* (2010) used an education measure for this category of effect. In Tables 3.17 and 3.18, we report the level of education measured by the percentage of the population who have completed primary school and the percentage who have a bachelor's degree or higher qualification, and classify the data according to the SAI model and the type of audits conducted. The countries with the highest education levels use the board/collegial model, followed by the Westminster model. Greater levels of education are associated with less use of the court model.

Table 3.17 Education levels and SAI model

SAI model	*Count of jurisdiction*	*Mean primary*	*Mean bachelor's*
Board/collegial	22	94.53	21.85
Board/collegial and Court/judicial	6	89.86	22.96
Board/collegial and Other institutional model	1	–	–
Court/judicial	5	62.51	12.34
Court/judicial and Part of Ministry of Finance and Other institutional model	1	–	–
Other institutional model	6	43.71	20.54
Westminster	50	82.37	20.40
Westminster and Court/judicial model	1	87.54	14.64
Westminster and Other institutional model	2	63.15	9.00
Not available	141	76.91	18.08
Grand total/Mean	**235**	80.01	19.18

Primary: Percentage of the population completing primary education (World Bank).
Bachelor's: Percentage of the population with bachelor's or higher degree (World Bank).

Table 3.18 Mean education levels and types of auditing

Types of audit	*Number of jurisdictions*	*Primary*	*Bachelor's*
Financial audits/Compliance audits	9	88.19	16.35
Financial audits/Compliance audits/ Performance audits	80	82.56	20.14
Financial audits/Performance audits	4	100.00	28.65
Compliance audits/Performance audits	1	80.28	16.54
Not available	141	76.58	17.92
Grand total/Mean	235	80.01	19.18

In Table 3.18, we examine education levels and types of auditing. There is also a pattern here, where higher levels of education are associated with the use of only financial audits and performance audits. However, the picture is mixed for the next highest levels of education – countries with higher percentages of people completing primary education are more likely to conduct only financial audits and compliance audits, while countries with more degree-level education are more likely to have an SAI that conducts all three types. Degree-level education is likely to be a more relevant measure of normative isomorphism that would have an impact on SAIs.

INTOSAI itself provides a high level of influence on SAIs, and that is likely to lead to an increased level of normative isomorphism. As an umbrella organisation for the SAI community, INTOSAI and its regional organisations operate a number of committees and working groups to monitor and advance professionalism in external government audit. Since 2004 INTOSAI has instigated a standard-setting board and International Standards for Supreme Audit Institutions (ISSAIs) to develop an "authoritative framework for public sector auditing".[8] Figure 3.2 lists the current standards on issue.

Further, INTOSAI seeks to develop capacity in SAIs through, inter alia, regional forums, promoting peer reviews and cooperative audits which enable best practices to be shared, through the *International Journal of Government Auditing* and conferences.[9] The Congress (INCOSAI) is held triennially and, since 2001, has resulted in 'Accords' summarising the findings of the Congress (e.g. 2001 resulted in the 'Seoul Accords'). In addition, INTOSAI has convened a Knowledge Sharing Committee (KSC) which aims to generate and disseminate knowledge amongst SAIs through such things as communities of practice, task forces and working groups.

In addition, in 1986 INTOSAI established the INTOSAI Development Initiative (IDI), and from 1999 it has operated as a separate legal entity

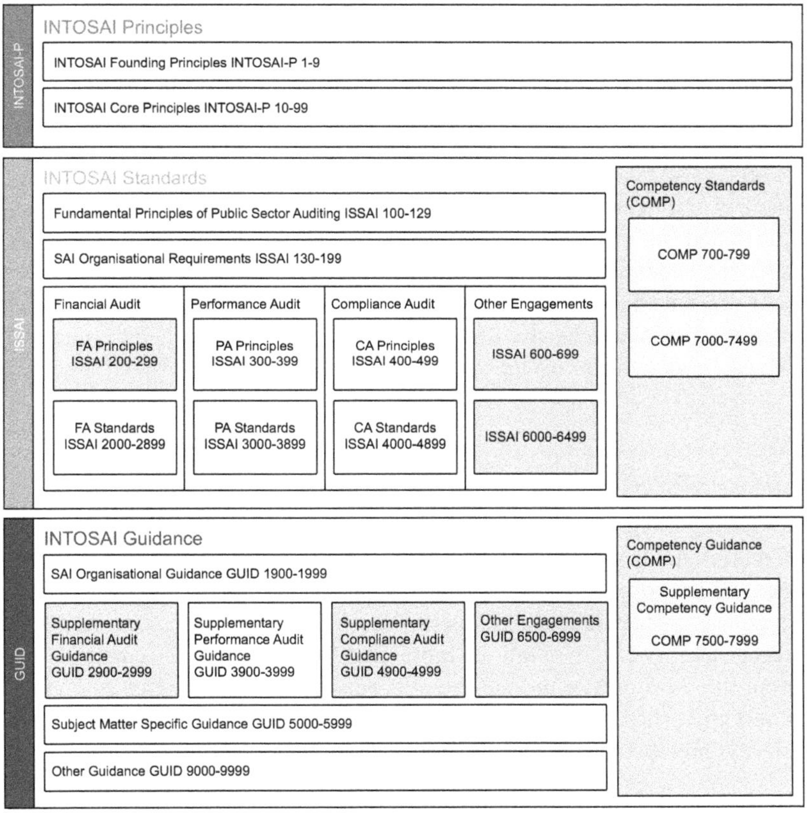

Figure 3.2 INTOSAI Principles, Standards and Guidance

Source: Taken from www.issai.org/professional-pronouncements/8 June 2020

registered in Norway. Its mission is to support SAIs to strengthen their performance and capacities, and one way it does this is through the Performance Measurement Framework (PMF).[10] This has been developed since 2012, piloted and endorsed by the XXIII INCOSAI in 2016. IDI has a number of reports on the use of the PMF in different nations and regions on its website. For example, PASAI reports on the PMF facilitation programme within the Pacific Region where a two-stage approach was taken. The first stage prioritised self-assessment and the second prioritised peer assessment. A coordinated approach was taken to analysing the capacity and performance of 11 SAIs within the region, with the balance of nine to be undertaken in the future. It is noted that the SAI PMF "can be used both for identification of needs, and as a measurement and monitoring tool" (INTOSAI PMF, 2016). The IDI recognises that such assessments can be internal, use peer assessment, external assessors or a hybrid of all approaches in order to provide details of an SAI's strengths and weaknesses and their influence on SAI performance (INTOSAI PMF, 2016). INTOSAI's IDI also publishes a triennial stocktaking report (INTOSAI IDI Development Initiative, 2017) which reports on SAI capacities and performance. The 2017 report concluded that "there is gradual adoption of the ISSAIs and slow but improving implementation" and, for example, that 72% of 102 SAIs surveyed were categorised as having "adequate" independence in 2015 (71% in 2012).

At present, the IDI website lists four countries or regional SAI bodies which have undergone the PMF. They are Bhutan, Brazil, Palestine and PASAI.[11] We are also aware that New Zealand has gone through the PMF exercise.[12] The influence of the PMF is likely to increase.

3.4.4 Summary of isomorphism

Reviewing the influences towards isomorphism shows that there are some effects but not from all of the isomorphic forces. We did not find evidence of coercive isomorphism having an effect through aid, debt or stock markets. There was some evidence of mimetic isomorphism because countries which lacked stability or rule of law are more likely to emulate stable countries and adopt the Westminster model. There is consistent evidence that normative isomorphism has an effect, with professional accounting, the level of education and membership of regional SAI groups having an impact.

3.5 Explanations for the existence of auditing, SAI model and types of auditing

The six explanations for the value of auditing that could potentially be applied to public sector auditing are agency costs, signalling, insurance, governance, management and confirmation of previous unaudited information (Hay and Cordery, 2018). Of those, agency costs and signalling are the most widely researched. We considered the impact of the existence of agency relationships, through democratic elections that hold officials to account and competition among political parties. We also considered the existence of a federal government structure as a potential source of agency costs and considered government borrowing as a measure of possible benefits from high-quality auditing by means of signalling.

The measures we used were the list of which countries are electoral democracies, from Freedom House (Freedom House, 2018), and World Bank measures from the Database of Political Institutions (World Bank, 2019). We used data codes for the World Bank Database of Political Institutions as explained in an earlier publication (Beck *et al*., 2001). We used the legislative index of electoral competition (LIEC) as our measure of political competition and the measure of whether subnational governments have extensive taxing, spending or regulatory authorities (AUTH) as a measure of whether there are federal government structures, both from the Database of Political Institutions.

Table 3.19 shows that the countries for which we have data are more likely to be electoral democracies and have higher electoral competition than those for which we do not. The six countries using a combined board/collegial and court/judicial model have lower scores on both measures, but the differences are still small, and most countries in our data have the maximum score. There is a tendency for countries where subnational governments have extensive authority to use the combined board/collegial and court/judicial model, or a model classified as 'Other'. The Westminster model is therefore associated with agency relationships only at a national level, between voters and government but not between different levels of government.

The number of audits carried out can also be seen as an agency measure, representing the number of agency relationships for which accountability

Table 3.19 Mean of measures of democracy, political competition, federal government and model of SAI

SAI model	*Count of jurisdiction*	*Freedom House electoral democracies*	*LIEC (electoral competition)*	*AUTH (subnational governments)*
Board/collegial	22	0.80	6.56	0.28
Board/collegial and Court/judicial	6	0.67	6.00	0.50
Board/collegial and Other institutional model	1	1.00	7.00	–
Court/judicial	5	0.75	7.00	0.33
Court/judicial and Part of Ministry of Finance and Other institutional model	1	–	4.00	–
Other institutional model	6	0.80	6.67	0.67
Westminster	50	0.78	6.36	0.21
Westminster and Court/judicial model	1	1.00	7.00	–
Westminster and Other institutional model	2	0.50	5.50	–
Not available	141	0.42	–	–
Total/Mean	96	0.56	6.23	0.25

through an audit is required. Table 3.20 reports the average number of audits conducted, classified by the SAI model. The results are quite striking, showing that the jurisdictions using the Westminster model have a relatively low number of audits compared to most other categories. This is surprising when compared to the results of Table 3.19. It may be that the Westminster model is more often chosen by countries where there are a relatively small number of agency relationships, and this result implies that this model is more suited to less complex settings.

The other explanation for the value of auditing that we can examine is signalling. Auditing is believed to be of value to entities because it provides a signal of higher accounting quality, and this will be attractive to potential investors (Titman and Trueman, 1986; Hay and Cordery, 2018). If this explanation applies at the country level, then we would expect jurisdictions with relatively higher borrowing to have good reasons to have more or better auditing. Borrowing is examined earlier in this chapter, in Table 3.9. That table shows that borrowing is highest in countries that use a board/collegial model. This result is driven by a few high-income countries that also have high debt per head (especially Germany and Switzerland). Westminster countries have a much smaller level of average debt, but there is also a much wider extent of variation among them in terms of debt and income.

Table 3.21 reports debt per head, but there are many missing observations. The level of debt is closely related to the overall wealth of the country, so the average tends to be lower in Westminster model countries, which include a wide range of both developed and developing economies.

Table 3.20 Number of audits

SAI model	*Number of observations*	*Mean number of audits conducted during the year*
Board/collegial	22	1,441
Board/collegial and Court/judicial	6	438
Board/collegial and Other institutional model	1	198
Court/judicial	5	568
Court/judicial and Part of Ministry of Finance and Other institutional model	1	161
Other institutional model	6	8,303
Westminster	50	396
Westminster and Court/judicial model	1	885
Westminster and Other institutional model	2	1,146
Grand total/Mean	94	1,224

Table 3.21 SAI model and debt per head

SAI model	*Count of debt/ head*	*Mean of debt/head (US dollars)*
Board/collegial	14	11,202
Board/collegial and Court/judicial	3	3,290
Board/collegial and Other institutional model	1	224
Court/judicial	3	1,024
Court/judicial and Part of Ministry of Finance and Other institutional model	1	1,131
Other institutional model	3	72,027
Westminster	33	9,939
Westminster and Court/judicial model	1	9,968
Westminster and Other institutional model	1	1,296
Not available	89	3,366
Grand total/Mean	149	6,886

3.6 Size and culture

Other variables not previously examined that might be important are the size of a country and its economy and cultural variables. Size could be important to many of the explanations – larger countries are more likely to have more levels of public sector management, and so more agency costs; on the other hand, they may be less subject to the forces that drive coercive and mimetic and normative isomorphism.

We used World Bank measures of population and total GDP (in US dollars) as our size measures. Table 3.22 shows that countries using the Westminster model have lower GDP, followed by those applying the court/judicial model, while board/collegial model countries are the largest. Westminster countries and court/judicial model countries also have smaller populations than the court/judicial model countries. (Of the two largest countries, India is in the 'Other' category, and China in the 'Not available' figure.)

Cultural differences, using Hofstede's cultural characteristics, have been examined in accounting studies (e.g. Gray, 1988). Hofstede's measures are Power Distance, Individuality, Masculinity and Uncertainty Avoidance (Hofstede, 1980, 2001, 2005). They are based on a study of a multinational corporation. The measures are not without controversy (Baskerville, 2003) but are nevertheless widely used (e.g. Mohamed Adnan *et al*., 2018). According to Gray (1988), individualism is positively related to disclosure, while masculinity, power distance and uncertainty avoidance are negatively related to disclosure. These measures were also used in the study of the adoption of accounting standards referred to in the previous chapter (Judge *et al*., 2010).

Table 3.22 SAI model and mean size

Model	*Count of GDP*	*GDP*	*Population*
Board/collegial	21	678,802,276,972	39,127,052
Board/collegial and Court/judicial	6	823,107,272,904	60,769,993
Board/collegial and Other institutional model	1	3,739,577,973	7,650,154
Court/judicial	5	523,693,302,596	16,569,823
Court/judicial and Part of Ministry of Finance and Other institutional model	1	223,779,865,815	95,540,395
Other institutional model	6	557,115,898,089	228,936,339
Westminster	50	42,956,535,373	19,836,124
Westminster and Court/judicial model	1	277,746,457,910	18,729,160
Westminster and Other institutional model	2	97,585,847,307	10,692,558
Not available	134	361,991,406,593	31,681,990
Grand total	227	381,100,291,647	35,344,727

Table 3.23 SAI model and mean cultural characteristics

SAI model	*Number*	*Power distance, mean*	*Individuality*	*Masculinity*	*Uncertainty avoidance*
Board/collegial	11	59.5	45.5	53.6	69.5
Board/collegial and Court/judicial	5	64.0	45.6	44.2	89.0
Board/collegial and Other institutional model	1	77.0	20.0	46.0	54.0
Court/judicial	2	67.0	45.0	41.5	90.0
Other institutional model	2	55.5	58.0	63.0	49.0
Westminster	21	50.4	42.9	49.4	59.9
Westminster and Court/judicial model	1	63.0	23.0	28.0	86.0
Westminster and Other institutional model	2	87.5	22.0	44.5	84.5
Not available	25	62.0	43.6	51.4	61.8
Grand total/Mean	70	59.2	43.0	50.1	65.7

The scores for Hofstede's cultural dimensions (as reported in Clearly Cultural, 2019) are used for the next analysis. Table 3.23 shows that there are substantial cultural differences, when this measure is used, among the countries that use different SAI models. The court model is used in countries high on power distance, low on masculinity and high on uncertainty avoidance. There is not much difference on the scores for individuality. The results suggest that the court model is suited to a particular cultural environment.

3.7 Effectiveness

A useful question to examine is which SAI model is most effective. This has been measured in a previous study by government expenditure, government effectiveness, production and corruption (Blume and Voigt, 2011). The previous studies have concluded that the court model is the least effective (Blume and Voigt, 2011; Johnsen, 2019). However, the countries using this model tend to be geographically concentrated and to have some other similar factors such as culture and the number of levels of government. It may be the case that the court model is adapted to certain settings, which for other reasons do not score well on models such as that of Blume and Voigt, and that the court model is in fact the most effective in some settings.

Blume and Voigt measured the effectiveness of SAIs in a number of ways. They argue that with an effective SAI, government expenditure should be lower, governmental effectiveness should be higher and the level of productivity in the economy should be higher. They acknowledge that their conjectures "paint a fairly optimistic view of the possibility of SAIs not only to monitor the behaviour of many government bodies but also to contribute substantially to the improvement of their behaviour" (Blume and Voigt, 2011, p. 217). This is certainly the case, and there are many other variables that are likely to influence these measures more strongly than government auditing does. However, as Blume and Voigt point out, some SAIs make claims of this kind, especially the UK National Audit Office which claims to save "millions of pounds" each year. Blume and Voigt also point out limitations on the ability of SAIs to achieve these benefits, one of which is the issue of SAIs themselves acting as self-interested agents who do not have very strong incentives to work hard. Blume and Voigt therefore examine the association between SAI variables and measures, including government expenditure, tax revenue, government effectiveness and corruption, and productivity, with control variables.

Blume and Voigt see freedom of the press in a country as a complementary mechanism to SAIs. In countries where the media are free to publicise SAI findings, then bureaucrats are more likely to pay attention to the findings of auditors (Blume and Voigt, 2011, p. 218). The SAI institutional details that Blume and Voigt consider are whether the mandate of the SAI is for ex-ante or ex-post auditing (which is similar to compliance audits versus financial audits), independence, measured by the constitutional protections for the SAI and including the SAI model, and finally the number of the SAI's employees.

Their results show that there is no association with the expected effects on the economy, with one exception: the court model of SAI is associated with a higher level of corruption. There is also an association between the court model and reduced government effectiveness in univariate analysis, but not when control variables are included. Blume and Voigt assume exogeneity, that factors like corruption of government effectiveness do not themselves influence the SAI model or other variables. However, it is plausible to expect that factors like this have had an influence on the SAI model and other related structural effects.

We have not examined the Blume and Voigt measures for overall government expenditure, tax, efficiency or productivity, as these associations seem to be giving the SAI too much importance in an economy, and their results do not generally support these measures. However, we have included government effectiveness.

An effectiveness measure is the percentage of firms identifying corruption as a major constraint, obtained from the World Bank economic surveys. The results of analysis of that survey and SAI model are shown in Table 3.29 (columns 2 and 3). The results show that, as Blume and Voigt conclude, the court model countries appear to have a higher level of corruption than the other groups.

Public corruption is measured by another World Bank indicator and is defined as "Control of Corruption captures perceptions of the extent to which public power is exercised for private gain, including both petty and grand forms of corruption, as well as 'capture' of the state by elites and private interests". The results are shown in columns 4 and 5 of Table 3.24, on a scale from –2.5 (most corrupt) to +2.5 (least corrupt). There are substantial differences, with the court model countries showing as most corrupt, the Westminster countries as having a positive score indicating less corruption, and the board model countries as least corrupt. The Westminster countries show substantial variation within the group.

Governmental effectiveness is defined in a World Bank survey as "perceptions of the quality of public services, the quality of the civil service and the degree of its independence from political pressures, the quality of policy formulation and implementation, and the credibility of the government's commitment to such policies". The scores are summarised by model in Table 3.25. The score is again measured on a scale from –2.5 to +2.5. For this measure the differences among the SAI models are quite clear. Court model countries have the least effective governments, Westminster model countries have a small positive score and board model countries are shown as having the highest quality of public services in terms of avoiding

Table 3.24 Mean of firms identifying corruption, public corruption and SAI model

SAI model	*Count of identifying corruption*	*Identifying corruption*	*Count of public corruption*	*Public corruption*
Board/collegial	12	30.75	20	0.41
Board/collegial and Court/judicial	3	56.57	6	0.24
Board/collegial and Other institutional model	1	45.50	1	–0.49
Court/judicial	3	50.63	4	–0.12
Court/judicial and Part of Ministry of Finance and Other institutional model	1	7.60	1	–0.49
Other institutional model	3	26.57	5	0.51
Westminster	34	34.07	50	0.21
Westminster and Court/judicial model	1	17.50	1	1.01
Westminster and Other institutional model	1	62.00	2	–0.56
Not available	85	43.03	133	–0.20
Grand total/Mean	144	39.72	223	–0.02

Source: World Bank, Enterprise Surveys Project (www.enterprisesurveys.org/Data/Explore Topics/corruption)

Table 3.25 Mean governmental effectiveness

SAI model	*Count of GOVEFF*	*GOVEFF*
Board/collegial	20	0.616
Board/collegial and Court/judicial	6	0.369
Board/collegial and Other institutional model	1	–1.143
Court/judicial	4	–0.252
Court/judicial and Part of Ministry of Finance and Other institutional model	1	–0.003
Other institutional model	5	0.461
Westminster	50	0.194
Westminster and Court/judicial model	1	1.084
Westminster and Other institutional model	2	–0.385
Not available	131	–0.233
Grand total/Mean	221	–0.025

corruption. This government effectiveness measure was also used by Blume and Voigt (2011), and they found a similar association, although their result does not hold in their multivariate tests.

Table 3.26 analyses the government effectiveness results according to the types of audit carried out. Compliance audits appear to be associated with lower effectiveness, and financial audits and performance audits with higher effectiveness.

The results examining government effectiveness are fairly consistent with Blume and Voigt. Countries that use the court model have more corruption and less effective governments. However, the direction of the cause and effect is not clear – do they have more corruption because the court model permits this? Or is it the opposite: countries that have more corruption choose the court model to help address the problem? Either alternative is consistent with the data.

Transparency is another measure of effectiveness. The Corruption Perceptions Index (CPI) produced by Transparency International is a widely used measure of a country's level of transparency. That index provides another measure of the effectiveness of an SAI, if it is assumed that the SAI can have an effect on the outcome.

The results shown in Table 3.27 of an analysis of the Corruption Perceptions Index and the SAI model do not show a pattern of an association between SAI model and transparency. The scores for each of the Westminster model, board model and court model are not very different. The detailed results showed very wide variations within each category.

Another measure of the effectiveness of an SAI is financial accountability within a country. The IFAC public sector financial accountability index is a measure of this and is reported in Table 3.28.

Table 3.26 Governmental effectiveness and type of audit

Type of audit	*Count of GOVEFF*	*GOVEFF*
Compliance audits/Performance audits	1	–0.447
Financial audits/Compliance audits	9	–0.123
Financial audits/Compliance audits/ Performance audits	76	0.270
Financial audits/Performance audits	4	1.640
Not available	131	–0.239
Grand total/Mean	221	–0.025

Table 3.27 Mean transparency and SAI model

SAI model	*Count of CPI 2018 Transparency International*	*CPI 2018 Transparency International*
Board/collegial	19	53.79
Board/collegial and Court/judicial	6	50.00
Board/collegial and Other institutional model	1	30.00
Court/judicial	4	43.00
Court/judicial and Part of Ministry of Finance and Other institutional model	1	33.00
Other institutional model	3	60.67
Westminster	43	48.98
Westminster and Court/judicial model	1	67.00
Westminster and Other institutional model	2	34.00
Not available	113	38.51
Grand total/Mean	193	43.17

Table 3.28 IFAC public sector financial accountability index

SAI model	*IFAC public sector financial accountability index*					
	Accrual	*Cash*	*Cash transitioning to accrual*	*Missing*	*Other*	*Grand total*
Board/collegial	5	5	7	1	–	18
Board/collegial and Court/judicial	3	–	2	1	–	6
Board/collegial and Other institutional model	–	–	1	–	–	1
Court/judicial	1	1	2	–	–	4
Court/judicial and Part of Ministry of Finance and Other institutional model	–	–	1	–	–	1
Other institutional model	2	2	1	–	–	5
Westminster	16	12	15	7	–	50
Westminster and Court/judicial model	–	–	1	–	–	1
Westminster and Other institutional model	–	–	1	1	–	2
Not available	11	38	35	37	3	124
Grand total	38	58	66	47	3	212

IFAC public sector financial accountability index from: www.ifac.org/what-we-do/global-impact-map/accountability (obtained 29/1/2020)

The results in Table 3.28 do not show differences among the various SAI models. There is no apparent association, and each model is about equally likely to use cash accrual or cash transitioning to accrual. However, there are few observations of court model countries in the data.

We also examine the type of audit using the IFAC index in Table 3.29.

There is not much data about type of audit and the public sector financial accountability index. The data that we have, in Table 3.29, suggest that compliance audits tend to be used in countries that use cash accounting, not accrual.

Another measure is adoption of International Public Sector Accounting Standards (IPSAS). The ACCA study (ACCA, 2017) examines progress in adopting IPSAS in a sample of developing countries in different regions of the world. The report concludes that there is evidence that IPSAS leads to greater accountability and transparency, better decision-making and other advantages (p. 5). Of the countries for which data is available, most were using the Westminster model, a lesser number using the board model and very few using the court model. The results (Table 3.30) show that the countries using the Westminster model mostly use IPSAS, and fewer of the board countries do. However, there is a limitation to these results because the countries examined were not chosen randomly and may have been selected after taking their SAI model into account.

As Table 3.31 shows, most of the countries in the study conducted all three: compliance audits, financial audits and performance audits. Since

Table 3.29 Type of audit and public sector financial accountability index

Types of audit	*IFAC public sector financial accountability index*					
	Accrual	*Cash*	*Cash transitioning to accrual*	*Missing*	*Other*	*Grand total*
Compliance audits/ Performance audits	–	–	1	–	–	1
Financial audits/ Compliance audits	1	3	2	3	–	9
Financial audits/ Compliance audits/ Performance audits	21	17	29	7	–	74
Financial audits/ Performance audits	4	–	–	–	–	4
Not available	12	38	34	37	3	124
Grand total	38	58	66	47	3	212

Table 3.30 ACCA study of IPSAS implementation

SAI model	*IPSAS implementation*					
	Adopted	*In progress*	*Not started*	*Partial*	*Planned*	*Grand total*
Board/collegial	1	1	1	1	–	4
Board/collegial and Court/judicial	–	1	–	–	–	1
Board/collegial and Other institutional model	–	–		–	–	–
Court/judicial	–	–	–	–	–	–
Court/judicial and Part of Ministry of Finance and Other institutional model	–	1	–	–	–	1
Other institutional model	–	–	1	–	–	1
Westminster	3	5	1	1	1	11
Westminster and Court/judicial model	–	1	–	–	–	1
Westminster and Other institutional model	–	1	–	–	–	1
Not available	4	3	–	2	–	9
Grand total	8	13	3	4	1	29

Table 3.31 IPSAS implementation and types of audits

Types of audit	*IPSAS implementation*					
	Adopted	*In progress*	*Not started*	*Partial*	*Planned*	*Grand total*
Compliance audits/ Performance audits	–	1	–	–	–	1
Financial audits/ Compliance audits		–	1	–	–	1
Financial audits/ Compliance audits/ Performance audits	4	9	2	2	1	18
Financial audits/ Performance audits	–	–	–	–	–	–
Not available	4	3	–	2	–	9
Grand total	8	13	3	4	1	29

they conducted performance audits, it is likely that their public sector accounting and auditing is relatively advanced.

3.8 Public value

Cordery and Hay (2019) report on how SAIs demonstrate that they are delivering value. INTOSAI standards encourage SAIs to recognise their value that they contribute to citizens, legislators and other stakeholders. Cordery and Hay examine the information that SAIs make available. The data is available for only 16 countries but nevertheless provide some insight.

The countries scoring most highly on having a strategic plan to deliver public value were New Zealand, the UK, the US, Australia and Canada – all countries that use a Westminster model, although they also have many other similarities and are likely to be influenced by each other. The countries with low scores are Norway, Switzerland, Iceland and Poland, but overall Cordery and Hay (2019) show that few SAIs explicitly discuss value, and of those that do, not all produce annual reports, and fewer publish annual and strategic plans. The countries studied were a diverse group, but of the 16 countries analysed, only Switzerland did not use the Westminster model (see Table 3.1 – it uses an 'Other institutional model').

3.9 Discussion and conclusion

This chapter has analysed data about SAIs using a wide variety of sources. We have attempted to examine both the factors that influence the model of SAI in a country and the types of audits as well as the effectiveness of the SAI using a range of measures. Issues that arose in carrying out this work included data problems. It is very difficult to obtain complete information about SAIs or about other factors related to countries, and nearly all of the figures that are included are incomplete. In addition, the information obtained is not always consistent. For example, the model of SAI can be classified in different ways and varies between sources such as previous research and INTOSAI data. Nevertheless, there are clear patterns that emerge.

In previous research, it has been found that SAIs can be classified into a small number of categories and that the court model is the least effective. Our analysis provides data that challenge these conclusions. When SAIs speak for themselves, in the INTOSAI survey, they use a much wider range of classifications and often choose to classify themselves as containing elements of more than one model.

We also found that SAIs vary more than the three- or four-type category used in previous research suggests. Nevertheless, if a simple classification is required, then the court model versus other models is probably the most useful because the court model appears to have the most differences in factors leading to its adoption, compared to the other models. It also varies more in the outcomes associated with it. A fourth category examined in some previous research, an audit function within the Ministry of Finance, appears to no longer generally apply.

There are some signs of isomorphism, especially mimetic isomorphism, which is evident in the large number of countries adopting the Westminster model. In many of these cases, the Westminster model is not consistent with their colonial history, and there appears to be a trend whereby this model has become a widely used standard model adopted by countries that are subject to isomorphic influences. Our data shows little evidence of coercive isomorphism but some influence from mimetic and normative isomorphism. Lower stability and reduced rule of law are associated with the court model. Education levels and membership of a regional SAI group are normative influences that are associated with the Westminster model.

However, few larger countries use the Westminster model, unless they do so for historic reasons, and it may be that the Westminster model is one that can be readily adopted by smaller jurisdictions with fewer audits and simpler systems of government. Our evidence shows that countries using the Westminster system tend to have fewer levels of government, carry out fewer audits and have smaller populations. The variables are associated with the value SAIs deliver in terms of at least agency theory, although the findings about signalling theory are less strong.

Previous research (e.g. Blume and Voigt, 2011) assumes that the SAI models are exogenous, perhaps because each country has its model for historic reasons that are not connected with present needs. However, it seems more likely that models have been selected with some regard to what is needed in each jurisdiction. It therefore may be the case that the court model is the most effective in countries where corruption is a high risk and is selected by these countries for that reason. The court model is associated with cultural influences and with higher levels of corruption.

When we examined the political stability data more closely, we also saw that the Westminster model includes countries with a much wider range of scores, including countries that are among the most stable such as New Zealand and Iceland, as well as more unstable countries including Ethiopia and Venezuela. The other categories do not include such extreme observations. This is consistent with the proposition that the Westminster model exists in stable countries and is the most widely used, and so it is emulated by those which are less stable, in a process of mimetic isomorphism. The results for mean political stability and mean political rights show a similar pattern, with the court/judicial jurisdictions showing higher average scores, representing reduced political rights and civil liberties.

In recent years, the influence of INTOSAI has increased. INTOSAI's standards and its development of a Performance Measurement Framework for SAIs has led them to pay greater attention to their work and to international best practice, and this is likely to lead to increased normative isomorphism.

The chapter includes some novel findings as set out earlier, including some surprising results. There are a wider range of SAIs than previous studies suggest. There are isomorphic and cultural effects. While previous research suggests that the court model is the least effective, our results imply that it may be the most suitable model for some jurisdictions. We also briefly discussed research on the public value of SAIs, but court model SAIs were not included in that research.

Further research on these issues will be worthwhile. In particular data from a wider range of countries would be helpful. And more analysis including multivariate tests will be useful. We now turn to consider the risks and opportunities in the future for SAIs.

Notes

1 The United Kingdom itself uses a term like this instead of 'Westminster' (European Court of Auditors, 2019).
2 Blume and Voigt classify these countries as using the court model: Bolivia, El Salvador, France, Greece, Italy, Norway, the Philippines, Romania, South Korea, Spain and Turkey. Their list varies considerably from Tables 3.1 and 3.2.
3 According to ISSAI 100 (ISSAI, 2019), "The three main types of public-sector audit are defined as follows: Financial audit focuses on determining whether an entity's financial information is presented in accordance with the applicable financial reporting and regulatory framework. Performance audit focuses on whether interventions, programmes and institutions are performing in accordance with the principles of economy, efficiency and effectiveness and whether there is room for improvement. Compliance audit focuses on whether a particular subject matter is in compliance with authorities identified as criteria. Compliance auditing is performed by assessing whether activities, financial transactions and information are, in all material respects, in compliance with . . . rules, laws and regulations, budgetary resolutions, policy, established codes, agreed terms or the general principles governing sound public-sector financial management and the conduct of public officials".
4 One of them, the United Kingdom, uses the terms 'financial and value-for-money'.
5 See also Kontogeorga (2018).
6 This could be stated as 'entities benefitting from public generosity' which included 'public finds granted to private entities, funds used by charities if they are donated through public campaigns and funds used by private entities if they are received by subsidiaries of any of these entities'; or just simply stated as 'Civil Society Organisations, Non-Government Organisations'.

7 The data was obtained from https://scholar.harvard.edu/files/shleifer/files/data_for_web.xls. Site accessed 15 November 2019.
8 www.intosai.org/what-we-do/professional-standards
9 www.intosai.org/what-we-do/capacity-development
10 www.idi.no/en/idi-cpd/sai-pmf
11 www.idi.no/en/idi-cpd/sai-pmf
12 https://oag.parliament.nz/2016/sai-pmf

References

ACCA (2017) *IPSAS Implementation: Current Status and Challenges*. Association of Chartered Certified Accountants, London.

Baker, C. R., Bédard, J. and Prat dit Hauret, C. (2014) 'The regulation of statutory auditing: An institutional theory approach', *Managerial Auditing Journal*, 29(5), pp. 371–394.

Baskerville, R. F. (2003) 'Hofstede never studied culture', *Accounting, Organizations and Society*, 28(1), pp. 1–14.

Beck, T., Clarke, G., Groff, A., Keefer, P. and Walsh, P. (2001) 'New tools in comparative political economy: The database of political institutions', *The World Bank Economic Review*, 15(1), pp. 165–176.

Blume, L. and Voigt, S. (2011) 'Does organizational design of supreme audit institutions matter? A cross-country assessment', *European Journal of Political Economy*, 27(2), pp. 215–229.

Bonollo, E. (2019) 'Measuring supreme audit institutions' outcomes: Current literature and future insights', *Public Money & Management*, 39(1), pp. 1–10.

Brown, P., Preiato, J. and Tarca, A. (2014) Measuring country differences in enforcement of accounting standards: An audit and enforcement proxy. *Journal of Business Finance and Accounting*, 41(1–2), pp. 1–52.

Clearly Cultural (2019) 'Geert Hofstede cultural dimensions', *Clearly Cultural: Making Sense of Cross Cultural Communication*. Available at: www.clearlycultural.com/geert-hofstede-cultural-dimensions/.

Cordery, C. J. and Hay, D. C. (2019) 'Supreme audit institutions and public value: Demonstrating relevance', *Financial Accountability & Management*, 35(2), pp. 128–142.

Deloitte (2019) 'Use of IFRS by jurisdiction', *iasplus.com*. Available at: www.iasplus.com/en/resources/ifrs-topics/use-of-ifrs.

DiMaggio, P. J. and Powell, W. W. (1983) 'The iron cage revisited: Institutional isomorphism and collective rationality in organizational fields', *American Sociological Review*, 48(2), pp. 147–160.

Djankov, S., La Porta, R., Lopez-de-Silanes, F. and Shleifer, A. (2008) 'The law and economics of self-dealing', *Journal of Financial Economics*, 88(3), pp. 430–465.

European Court of Auditors (2019) *Public Audit in the European Union*. Luxembourg: Publications Office of the European Union.

Freedom House (2018) *Freedom in the World Data and Resources*. Available at: https://freedomhouse.org/content/freedom-world-data-and-resources.

Gray, S. J. (1988) 'Towards a theory of cultural influence on the development of accounting systems internationally', *Abacus*, 24(I), pp. 1–15.

Hay, D. C. and Cordery, C. J. (2018) 'The value of public sector audit: Literature and history', *Journal of Accounting Literature*, 40, pp. 1–15.

Heald, D. (2018) 'Transparency-generated trust: The problematic theorization of public audit', *Financial Accountability & Management*, pp. 1–19.

Hofstede, G. (1980) *Culture's Consequences: International Differences in Work-Related Values*. Beverly Hills, CA: Sage Publications.

Hofstede, G. (2001) *Culture's Consequences: Comparing Values, Behaviors, Institutions and Organizations Across Nations*. 2nd edn. Thousand Oaks, CA: Sage Publications.

Hofstede, G. (2005) *Cultures and Organizations: Software of the Mind*. 2nd edn. New York, NY: McGraw-Hill.

INTOSAI (2019) *SAI's Information Database*. Available at: www.intosai.org/sais-information-database.

INTOSAI IDI Development Initiative (2017) *Global Stocktaking Report 2017*. INTOSAI IDI Development Initiative, Norway.

INTOSAI PMF. (2016) *Supreme Audit Institutions Performance Measurement Framework October 2016*. INTOSAI IDI Development Initiative, Norway.

ISSAI (2019) *ISSAI 100: Fundamental Principles of Public-Sector Auditing*. International Organisation of Supreme Audit Institutions, Denmark.

Johnsen, Å. (2019) 'Public sector audit in contemporary society: A short review and introduction', *Financial Accountability & Management*, 35(2), pp. 121–127.

Judge, W., Li, S. and Pinsker, R. (2010) 'National adoption of international accounting standards: An institutional perspective', *Corporate Governance: An International Review*, 18(3), pp. 161–174.

Kontogeorga, G. N. (2018) 'Juggling between ex-ante and ex-post audit in Greece: A difficult transition to a new era', *International Journal of Auditing*, (October 2018), pp. 86–94.

Lamoreaux, P. T., Michas, P. N. and Schultz, W. L. (2015) 'Do accounting and audit quality affect World Bank lending?', *The Accounting Review*, 90(2), pp. 703–738.

La Porta, R., Lopez-De-Silanes, F. and Shleifer, A. (2006) 'What works in securities laws?', *Journal of Finance*, 61(1), pp. 1–32.

Mohamed Adnan, S., Hay, D. C. and van Staden, C. J. (2018) 'The influence of culture and corporate governance on corporate social responsibility disclosure: A cross country analysis', *Journal of Cleaner Production*, 198, pp. 820–832.

Moore, M. H. (2013) *Recognizing Public Value*. Cambridge, MA & London: Harvard University Press.

OECD (2012) *Good Practices in Supporting Supreme Audit Institutions*. OECD Publishing, Paris.

Pollitt, C. and Summa, H. (1997) 'Comparative and international administration reflexive watchdogs ? How supreme audit institutions account for themselves', *Public Administration*, 75, pp. 313–336.

Puddington, A. and Dunham, J. (2017) *Freedom in the World: The Vital Center*. New York, NY: Freedom House.

Skaaning, S.-E. (2010) 'Measuring the rule of law', *Political Research Quarterly*, 63(2), pp. 449–460.

Stapenhurst, R. and Titsworth, J. (2001) 'Features and functions of supreme audit institutions', *World Bank PREM-notes*. Poverty Reduction and Economic Management Network, Washington DC, USA.

TheGlobalEconomy.com (2019) *Political Stability by Country, around the World.* Available at: www.theglobaleconomy.com/rankings/wb_political_stability/%0A.

Titman, S. and Trueman, B. (1986) 'Information quality and the valuation of new issues', *Journal of Accounting and Economics*, 8, pp. 159–172.

World Bank (2019) 'Database of political institutions', *World Bank Data Catalog*. Available at: https://datacatalog.worldbank.org/dataset/wps2283-database-political-institutions.

4 Risks and opportunities in the future

4.1 Introduction

In Chapters 2 and 3, we outlined research and empirical data seeking to explain the differences between SAIs and the functions they undertake. In line with institutional theory (DiMaggio and Powell, 1983), we considered isomorphic pressures that may lead to similarities and differences. In this chapter we analyse environmental pressures (defined as 'trends') that could affect public sector audit as a whole, recognising that each SAI could respond differently to these trends. The future of public sector audit includes new ways of auditing and new 'things to audit' (e.g. blockchain or sustainability) and the opportunities these raise. As in prior chapters, this chapter draws on recent literature, the survey developed for this book and other sources. There are two parts to the chapter: in the first part we discuss the changes that are likely to occur due to particular trends, and in the second part we discuss the views of SAIs around the world that completed our survey.

In private sector auditing, there are frequent calls for change in the 'audit market', generally resulting from auditing scandals. An example is the flurry of reviews into the quality and effectiveness of private sector audit in the United Kingdom in late 2018 and 2019. They resulted from the failure of Carillion, Patisserie Valerie and London Capital and Finance and the ensuing impact on shareholders, bondholders, government and the public.[1] Other countries have also developed reviews of private sector audit for similar reasons, with the Australian Senate requiring the Parliamentary Joint Committee on Corporations and Financial Services to undertake an inquiry into the regulation of audit;[2] the Dutch Authority for Financial Markets exploring the "vulnerabilities" in the structure of the audit sector;[3] and CPA Canada Foresight seeking a new strategic direction for the audit profession through "reimagining",[4] to name responses by a few. The legitimacy of private sector audit is under question, as are the structures of the accounting firms that deliver audit. The Brydon call for views (see endnote 1) seeks to develop "a more useful and forward-looking audit". The Dutch are considering how audit can be of higher quality while CPA Canada is assessing how audit can keep ahead (or not fall behind) of the needs to measure performance in other than financial terms, to deal with 'Big Data' and to deal with new models of governance.

To date, recent private sector scandals appear usually to have passed over public sector audit. Previously we have argued that public sector audit adds value by being, inter alia, independent, high quality and useful to improve public sector practices (Cordery and Hay, 2018). Nevertheless, changes to the structure and composition of private sector audit are likely to impact the future of public sector audit as well and the value it can bring. This trend is especially likely as SAIs increasingly contract out to external (private sector) firms to deliver some of their audit services. In some countries (such as the UK) certain parts of the public sector can commission their own audits from private firms (see, for example, Ferry and Eckersley, 2015).

4.2 Future opportunities for audit

Future opportunities for audit will therefore draw on what the future holds. We recognise that the future will be different from today and that there is a number of different possible futures (Cuhls, 2003). There is also a status quo bias to any attempt to forecast the future (Susskind and Susskind, 2015). Nevertheless, a number of 'mega' trends can be considered when analysing future opportunities. Therefore, in this chapter we consider the main trends affecting the future of public audit, auditing and the accounting profession, as well as the environment in which public sector audit operates. As such, it is an attempt at foresight to use information gathered about future trends that enables implementations of potential new approaches for the present, or very near future (Cuhls, 2003). The format of the analysis can be visualised by Figure 4.1. Following the brief consideration of these trends, the practical ways in which SAIs are preparing for the future will be discussed.

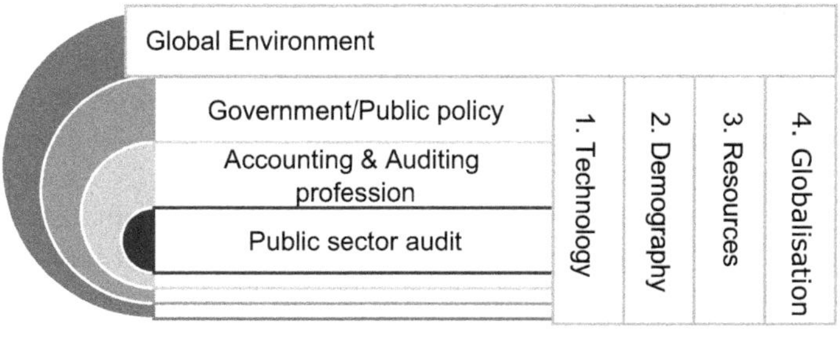

Figure 4.1 Different futures for public sector audit to consider

4.2.1 Global environment

A number of studies analyse data to assist nations, sectors and larger groups to discern trends that will impact the future of society. The most common trends are technology, demography, pressure on resources and globalisation affecting politics.

It is no surprise that **technology** is a major source of change that will affect the future (European Commission, 2012; Yeoman, 2012). Susskind and Susskind (2015) argue that exponential growth in information technology will lead to "increasingly capable machines, increasingly pervasive devices and increasingly connected humans". The rise of artificial intelligence (AI) is an example of capability, and Big Data enables new knowledge to be generated more quickly than ever before. We are also entering the age of global connectivity (European Commission, 2012) and of the 'internet of things'. This trend influences the future with increased transparency and (technically) readily available data to those who seek to analyse it (including public sector audit as discussed later). Nevertheless, the National Intelligence Council (2012) questions whether technological breakthroughs can occur quickly enough to assist in solving future issues.

In respect of **demography**, the rising population (predicted to be 9 billion worldwide by 2050), longer life expectancy, changing reproduction patterns and a greater proportion of the worldwide population living in Asia will disrupt our previous notions of population growth (European Commission, 2012; National Intelligence Council, 2012). There will also be more countries reaching the 'middle-income' levels at which saving for the future is feasible (World Bank Group, 2015). Those with increased wealth are likely to increase their investments for the future, including international investment, which will require regulation and careful management (Mowat Centre, 2014). Further, an increased population will stretch the world's resources (National Intelligence Council, 2012; Yeoman, 2012; Mowat Centre, 2014) and therefore increase the need for cooperation (see government/public policy in the next section).

Yet, not only will people live longer, but they are also likely to have more unequal access to wealth, more complex family structures and therefore greater diversity (Carney, 2014). This ageing population in an age with weaker family ties and greater inequality (within societies) will increase the pressure on public spending (European Commission, 2012). As an example, the COVID-19 pandemic has highlighted the high number of vulnerable people and demands by citizens for more personalised services (e.g. flights back to their home country from abroad, special consideration of their working environment and so on). This theme is picked up in the next section (public policy).

A third trend is the pressure on the world's **resources** and climate change. Hence, there is increased interest that future developments should be managed in such a way that they are environmentally friendly, curb excesses in consumerism and therefore that governments measure happiness beyond merely GDP (European Commission, 2012; National Intelligence Council, 2012). The National Intelligence Council (2012) notes that resource demand will require trade-offs between different resources. Global resource demands also require cooperation and collaboration.

Globalisation is not a new trend, but the increasing unpredictability of political developments is likely to mean that globalisation will assume a greater influence on future politics. Globalisation will be experienced heterogeneously in different regions (European Commission, 2012; National Intelligence Council, 2012; Mowat Centre, 2014). Nevertheless, the Mowat Centre (2014) also suggests that the future success of government will depend on "greater cooperation in the international arena" and interconnectedness.

These changes to the environment will affect government/public policy, as we now discuss.

4.2.2 Government/public policy

The Mowat Centre (2014) argues that government will need to be more proactive in engaging with citizens, promoting behavioural change and therefore mitigating the worst impacts from changes in the global environment, particularly citing ecosystems and the need to live sustainably. The National Intelligence Council (2012) questions whether governments are able to adapt sufficiently quickly to harness the positive aspects of change, and call the inability to do this "a game-changer". The influence of **technology**, especially social media but also the development of such systems as e-voting, will be felt particularly strongly in the political future. These will need to meet the challenge of low levels of trust in public institutions (Chartered Institute of Public Finance and Accountancy and Public Finance, 2005). Publicity about 'fake news' shows that citizens find it hard to know who or what to trust, as governments and their departments seek to show themselves as trusted advisors. However, it is commonly believed that public sector audit can increase public trust.

Technological change not only means that movements such as e-government will lead to increased transparency but also that citizens will demand more evidence-based policy (Mowat Centre, 2014). Greater availability of the internet provides data and a forum for critiquing government actions and for a new breed of 'influencer'. Technological change also blurs the lines between the private and public spheres and highlights the increasing issue of cyber security which can lead to loss or publication of confidential data, as well as defrauding citizens. The ability of governments to regulate and manage the desire to be transparent and the threat of hacking remains a challenge for the future.

Demographic changes (and to some extent globalisation) have brought the need and demand for co-production of public services to citizens. We use the term co-production as an overarching term to encompass the range of responsibilities for the design and delivery of services, with full co-production perceived as occurring when professionals and communities both co-plan and co-deliver those public services (Ryan, 2012). Greater co-production (sometimes posited to be part of New Public Governance (NPG)) is perceived as a way to re-enfranchise citizens 'disempowered' from the excesses of NPM (Ryan, 2012). It recognises the rise of the individual (Mowat Centre, 2014) and is also a way to proactively engage with citizens in developing a better future.

Resources have two main impacts on public policy and governments discussed here: climate change and public debt. In respect of climate change, there is therefore a need for governments to adapt systems to reduce climate change and to mitigate the effects of unpredictable weather events through building resilience. Regarding resource scarcity, there is also the need for good policies to better manage these resources, including water, energy, food and minerals (Mowat Centre, 2014). Again, collaborative policies to manage excesses and shortages will continue to be of importance (e.g. IMF Fiscal Affairs, 2020a). Of particular interest in environmental sustainability are the Sustainable Development Goals (SDGs) adopted by the United Nations and the way in which governments have willingly signed up to achieve these. There is some scepticism as to whether meaningful change will occur.

"Public debt is expected to operate as a significant constraint on fiscal and policy options through to 2030 and beyond" (Mowat Centre, 2014, p. 3). Higher levels of debt will ensue from the need for increased infrastructure to deal with environmental changes (e.g. from climate change), larger pension/social security payments to an ageing population (and higher health costs) and increased exposure to global risks. The IMF Fiscal Affairs (2020b) states that the fiscal responses by governments to the COVID-19 pandemic will likely have a sizeable impact on government budgets and debt. They note the need for transparent and fair policy measures, as well as risk mitigation. Nevertheless, the pandemic has had a severe impact on resources worldwide and may result in a larger public sector if more activities are taken over as a result of pandemics and other economic events.

Globalisation is increasing, and the effect of unstable governments both at home and abroad will impact public policy. Pöysti (2007) opines that the global public policy environment is one in which industrialised economies must innovate, while emerging economies are able to learn from prior innovations. Nevertheless, decisions taken by industrialised countries may also negatively impact emerging economies, especially when they impose restrictions and standards that emerging economies may not be able to meet.

These broad categories of government changes will have an impact on the accounting and auditing profession, as will general environmental changes, which are now discussed.

4.2.3 The accounting and auditing profession

Susskind and Susskind (2015) argue that we are entering a 'post-professional society' where expertise as institutionalised in the professions is being diminished through **technology** and the breakdown of regulatory barriers. The rise of technology points to a future that will increasingly see professional work reconfigured through new relationships and different ways of communicating. This dovetails with a predicted global trend towards business fragmentation and desire for individualism (PricewaterhouseCoopers, 2014). Automation and innovation are also expected to continue through the increased commoditisation of professional 'work' which should open up new roles for non-professionals and savvy professionals alike (Susskind and Susskind, 2015; Schwartz *et al.*, 2019). However, it is likely to lead to reduced trust in the profession as it now stands.

The rise of new forms of technology has enabled greater networking and collaboration of (online) providers and therefore reduces domination by an elite in a particular area. Financial statement auditing is particularly amenable to these developments. Rather than sampling transactions and details, new technologies allow for the total population of transactions to be tested (Susskind and Susskind, 2015). Many reconciliations and recalculations can be undertaken swiftly (Federation of European Accountants, 2014; KPMG Board Leadership Centre, 2018; Salijeni *et al.*, 2019). Indeed, artificial intelligence can also assist in identifying probability models to reduce error (Simon, 2019).

The networking and collaboration identified by Susskind and Susskind (2015) is also likely to extend to staff of auditees, who increasingly do not work 'in the office' but in alternative arrangements (Schwartz *et al.*, 2019). This issue reflects on the extent to which auditees can control staff and how auditors can gain visibility over internal controls if they do not have access to the auditees' workplace and staff. Despite technology, those involved in professional auditing continue to argue that human judgement will continue to be important (PricewaterhouseCoopers, 2019).

Nevertheless, auditors have been slow to respond to these technological changes (Salijeni *et al.*, 2019), with clients desiring them to 'look to the future' and perform a deeper analysis (Forbes Insights and KPMG, 2017, p. 6), in particular to signal risk (PricewaterhouseCoopers, 2019). Among the challenges is to use Big Data effectively (KPMG Board Leadership Centre, 2018; Salijeni *et al.*, 2019).

Demographic change will also affect the accounting and auditing workforce. In particular, studies show that future employees will have different demands of employers, particularly seeking flexible work and firms that are sustainable and can meet economic and social goals (PricewaterhouseCoopers, 2014). Greater ability to work from home is a present demand and one that is likely to lead to future structural changes in the workplace.

Growing **resource scarcity** and concerns about climate change have seen the rise of non-financial reporting, and this is likely to escalate. The challenges for the future are how to ensure this is reliable, comparable and auditable (PricewaterhouseCoopers, 2019; Hay, 2020). When the auditee is hit by an economic shock, there is greater reliance on the auditor to ensure that they appropriately assess the measurement and disclosures to ensure that the ongoing concern assumption is not challenged.

Globalisation is likely to affect the accounting and auditing profession in a number of ways. Three are highlighted here that are relevant to this study. The first is the expansion of readers/users of audit reports. Readers of audit reports are placing increasing demands on the transparency of reports, the frequency of reports and other methods of communication (Federation of European Accountants, 2014; Forbes Insights and KPMG, 2017; KPMG Board Leadership Centre, 2018). Calls for reform recognise the need for audit to be undertaken for a wider range of stakeholders, rather than merely shareholders (PricewaterhouseCoopers, 2019). However, Hay (2020) notes that increased investment in index-based funds brings the likelihood of smaller but more sophisticated audiences for audit reports. The expectation gap (Simon, 2019) is also applicable to the public sector (Grace *et al.*, 2012).

The second way in which globalisation affects accounting and the auditing profession is through the rise of blockchain, which enables alternatives to hard currency in the form of cryptocurrency. These transactions need to be audited for greater legitimacy (Hay, 2020). The third is joint audit, or the requirement for another auditor to double-check the auditor's work (Siddiqui, 2019; Hay, 2020). Siddiqui (2019) notes that the empirical evidence is equivocal on the effectiveness of joint audit and that it has little allure in jurisdictions where it is voluntary, especially given the higher cost of audit under such a regime.

4.2.4 Public sector audit

Barrett (1996, p. 141) observed, more than two decades ago, that "many auditors general are taking initiatives aimed at influencing the nature of [the corporate governance] system rather than simply being a watchdog over it". This links to the rise in performance auditing at a similar time, greater use of technology, communications and 'good practice' reports, as well as the more commercial environment in which SAIs now operate. It is apparent that public sector audit is impacted not only by general environmental changes and those in government/public policy but also those to the professions.

In respect of **technology**, various proponents of greater transparency in the public sector have suggested that crowdsourcing would open public documents to scrutiny to augment public sector audit (Susskind and Susskind, 2015). These have indicated that there will be a rise of 'armchair auditors' who will publicise failings in, for examples, local government data (Chartered Institute of Public Finance and Accountancy and Public Finance, 2005) or wider government data (O'Leary, 2015). Nevertheless, these announcements have been attended by scepticism that the public will be interested enough to utilise such data. Further, Grace *et al.* (2012) suggest that if they are, the public auditor must be responsive and analyse how they can benefit from these 'armchair auditors'. The areas in which citizens might be interested may not link directly to audit, and auditors need to have "expertise in social media, advanced data analysis, and data visualisation" to use it (Grace *et al.*, 2012, p. 28).

As noted, changing **demographics** should lead to greater co-production. This would reflect citizens' demands for personalised services and a desire for assurance as to the quality of these services (Chartered Institute of Public Finance and Accountancy and Public Finance, 2005). Gareth Davies (in CIPFA & Public Finance, 2005) predicts the continued rise of performance scores recorded by users of public services ('Trip Advisor-type' metrics) and demand for audit or verification of these. Further, while privatisation and public sector contracting-out has attended NPM reforms, co-production and public policy changes will increase cross-agency and cross-sector initiatives (Chartered Institute of Public Finance and Accountancy and Public Finance, 2005). These blur the lines of the 'public entity' and indeed the entity concept. New ways of auditing and refinement of audit mandate will be required in the future.

Performance reporting will need to develop to assist better use of **scarce resources**. The extent to which the public sector is prepared for greater risks and the manner in which SAIs can assist in managing those risks is currently questioned (Grace *et al.*, 2012). The challenge for SAIs is to "focus on the quality of governance . . . and the assurance of the quality of regulatory management" (Pöysti, 2007, p. 2). Nevertheless, Monroe-Ellis (2018) believes that cross-cutting performance audits are the way that SAIs can raise awareness of risks that governments may not be aware of – this may also involve critiquing policy.

Particular scarce resource issues include the need to appropriately assist environmental sustainability (Bititci *et al.*, 2012) and therefore the achievement of SDGs. Rajaguguk *et al.* (2017) also note the global nature of SDGs and the development of the INTOSAI framework for audit of the achievement of SDGs. They suggest this will need more cooperative audits (i.e. joint, coordinated or parallel audits) (see also ISSAI 5800 *Guide for Cooperative Audit Programs between Supreme Audit Institutions*[5] – still in draft at time of writing) to ensure global goals are met. Rajaguguk *et al.* (2017) also note that data for achieving such goals are likely to be held by more than one ministry and show a case study of how a consolidated audit report was prepared for a poverty reduction programme.

Scarce resources also extend to the growing public debt, as has been indicated in our earlier discussion. This suggests that public audit could be increasingly called upon to ensure fiscal controls are being adhered to and to call for fiscal policies that ensure prudent medium- to long-term planning (Grace *et al.*, 2012; Mowat Centre, 2014). With resources being increasingly offered to private sector operators, for example in the wake of the COVID-19 pandemic (e.g. IMF Fiscal Affairs, 2020b), the risk of fraud may be greater and require more forensic, rather than conventional, financial statement audit. And yet, recent research by Reichborn-Kjennerud *et al.* (2019) suggests that SAIs generally see the tasks of detecting and investigating such corruption/fraud as outside of their mandate. Governments' resourcing in the wake of the COVID-19 pandemic may result in more entities to audit and fewer resources to undertake the audits.

Measures to respond to resource scarcity may also result in SAIs being called upon to critique policy, despite previously having argued that this blurs their independence (Normanton, 1966; Grasso and Sharkansky, 2001). Another independence risk is responsiveness to stakeholders, as noted by Yamamoto and Kim (2019).

The future will also require SAIs to communicate more effectively about audit matters in a timely manner and in a way that connects with citizens and builds their trust (Chartered Institute of Public Finance and Accountancy and Public Finance, 2005; Pöysti, 2007).

Globalisation is likely to increase the uptake of different forms of public administration with wider use of NPM and development support from transnational entities (van Helden and Uddin, 2016). This has resulted in some homogenisation of forms of accounting (as shown in Chapter 3, with accrual accounting being increasingly used) but also many local diversifications and demands for information. Further, the call by Pöysti (2007) to innovate in public policy recognises the role of public sector auditors in enhancing reform and effectiveness (Monroe-Ellis, 2018; Johnsen *et al.*, 2019).

In addition, the need to collaborate across global (multicultural) networks will also disperse and change the performance measurement systems being used (Bititci *et al.*, 2012) and which need to be audited (Grace *et al.*, 2012; Federation of European Accountants, 2014). While Bititci *et al.* (2012) review literature analysing supply networks focused on value, co-production is an example of global networks in which governments participate. Bititci *et al.* (2012) suggest that performance measurement is increasingly moving from rational control towards cultural control and learning, and from discrete measurement to integrated measurement. It is not clear how public audit can respond to these fundamental shifts, but it would suggest that more flexible methods, as well as leadership, are required.

It is therefore apparent that there are many trends that act as pressures to change. Whether isomorphism will bring about similarities or whether SAIs will respond differently to these future trends cannot be answered at this stage.

4.3 What are SAIs preparing for?

As previously noted, we surveyed SAIs in respect of the future needs of stakeholders and different assurance services that they are developing in response to those. We received responses from 35 INTOSAI members across the world who are responsible for undertaking statutory audit for a wide range of public entities at national and local levels, as well as, in some cases, entities not in the public sector but that receive public money. They represented the spectrum of SAI types. Chapter 3 also shows that these SAIs used various standards to provide their audit services, with the great majority adopting or basing their standards on ISSAI. To inform this chapter, we asked specific questions, including "what impact do you think future events will have on your delivery of services?" and "why?", and then asking respondents to reflect on why stakeholders demand audit, and whether they believed that the reasons for stakeholders to demand audit would change in the future. SAI respondents were also asked "what particular challenges do you face currently?" and whether there were new assurance services that the SAI was developing for future use.

The survey responses show that respondents were aware of some but not all of the trends discussed in the previous sections. Performance auditing was the major area that was expected to be affected in the future (42%), followed equally by compliance audits and financial statement audits (29%).

Nevertheless, a small number of respondents thought that certain audits would not be affected by the future – compliance audits (two respondents) and financial statement and performance audits (one respondent each).

4.3.1 Stakeholders' demands for audit: demographic focus

All respondents agreed that stakeholders made demands for public sector audits. These demands were generally predicted to rise in the future. These changes could occur as part of changes in technology and demography, as noted:

> [Increased demand will occur] because of change in governance structures within government entities, corporate entities and change in technology.
>
> Demand for different types of audits (IT, Cybercrime, environment) may increase due to the composition of the population – millennial etc.

In particular these needs are likely to be related to future risks:

> The expectations and requirements of the stakeholders will also change in the very near future. It is expected that the SAIs have the competence and technical infrastructure to make more comprehensive analysis of public problems, based on data. It is expected that the SAI, based on the analysis of large volumes of information, can not only analyse descriptions but also projections of the risks or opportunities that could materialize.
>
> As long as risks increase, stakeholders' demands will increase.

Demands were expected to extend due to issues identified as arising from demography, scarce resources and globalisation:

> We believe that stakeholders will increasingly demand more value for money from public services and more equity in accessing these services. Thus, SAIs would be expected to ensure that best use is made of public funds.
>
> Stakeholders expect value for money on public sector expenditures.
>
> The stakeholders will be more interested in performance issues.

In addition, traditional issues of transparency and accountability were raised but with a recognition that global expectations of this would increase:

> There might be even more need for transparency.
>
> Stakeholders will continue to demand greater accountability from the public sector especially on the allocation of resources and implementation of programmes.

> Demands will change because donors and international agencies are demanding oversight and accountability and if assurance is not provided, then both audit and stakeholders' demands will change.
>
> There is an increasing demand for a better, greater and more public accountability of the public managers. As the external auditor, the [SAI] plays a major role in this process.

A number of respondents noted that it was necessary for legislation to reflect the needs of Parliament and other stakeholders to hold the government of the day to account. They further agreed that such legislation could change to respond to future needs and that it is necessary for the SAI to be prepared for these changes.

4.3.2 Stakeholders' demands for audit: technology focus

In preparation for these expected changes to stakeholders' expectations, SAIs are responding to technology change by, for example:

> [Developing] IT audits, audit of extractive industries, climate change funding reviews.
>
> [Undertaking] rapid case reviews.
>
> [Our] quality assurance process . . . appears to us as quite efficient. However, we are currently working in increasing our capacities in terms of the use of IT in the audit and quality control process.
>
> We are testing how we use data and information to provide better and more timely insights.
>
> We intend to introduce data analytics in our audit work. An internal audit team drawn from the various audit sections has been set up to analyse how data analytics can be implemented by [the SAI] in its audit work.
>
> [Our SAI] is now working on developing an electronic system for monitoring recommendations implementations. The system will ensure more proactive and intensive communication with our auditees and will give opportunity to continuously monitor the recommendations' implementation process.

Further, the role of demography and co-creation (co-production) was highlighted by one respondent:

> It is important that SAIs continue to apply innovation principles to:
>
> – Focus on people . . .

– Apply co-creation to participate to the different parties related to public problems.

4.3.3 Stakeholders' demands for audit: resources focus

Resource constraints, as recognised in stakeholders' demands for more value for money (as noted earlier) are also recognised in the design of new and different assurance products, for example:

> More performance audit on government programs and projects.
>
> Performance audits on the effectiveness of the measures for the fulfilment of the sustainable development objectives.
>
> The requirements of the sustainable development audit.

These mirror the call by the Jamaican Auditor-General (and General Secretary for the Caribbean Regional Organisation of INTOSAI (CAROSAI)) Pamela Monroe-Ellis (Monroe-Ellis, 2018) for SAIs to be determined enough to assist governments to deliver on their SDGs. In order to do this, SAIs are developing and following international best practice.

4.3.4 Stakeholders' demands for audit: globalisation focus

Globalisation, as also suggested previously, is being picked up in different ways by SAIs around the world. By some it is, as these responses show:

> Our office adopted the methodology of specific scope audits. The purpose of this methodology is to streamline audits by addressing one or two specific issues at a time.
>
> Taking up international Best Practice [through new] quality assurance standards for the [SAI].
>
> [Extending mandate to] certification of the annual accounts of the Federal State and all Federated entities (from 2020 at the latest).

The suggestion by Pöysti (2007) that industrialised nations must show the way to emerging economies was acknowledged by respondents who noted:

> [Some] SAIs are faced with unique challenges due to their geographical location and size. [INTOSAI's] regional organisations . . . and development partners such as . . . IDI have greatly contributed to the development of these SAIs and should continue with the good work.
>
> Governments in Africa should pay attention to the roles of oversight institutions.

Nevertheless, some smaller SAIs and those in countries where conflict has been severe may have unique challenges to face. For example, one respondent noted:

> In a post conflict country . . . where systems are being slowly rebuilt, implementation of audit recommendations by public sector entities is a challenge.

This reflects the unstable political environment in which the world increasingly finds itself. Dealing with these issues may take precedence over planning for other future global trends.

Further, although the questions in this part of the survey focused on the future and how this might impact the SAI and its work, some respondents reflected on current challenges to ensure independence and competent staff in order to ensure public value (Cordery and Hay, 2018). For example:

> Currently we are working on institutional development through continuous training. It is expected that the quality of service being provided will result in improved quality assurance.
>
> The SAI is engaged in capacity building of its staff through development partners to enhance their skills. That will improve their duties in the short and medium term.
>
> One of [our] strategic goals for the years 2019–2023: To become a leader in selected fields of public sector audit (such as environmental auditing) and to be acknowledged as a centre of excellence and expertise within the . . . public administration. We shall continue to work towards the improvement of the public service by adopting good practices in audit methodology and reporting, in line with established auditing standards, communicating better with stakeholders without impairing our independence, and providing a multidisciplinary professional service to Parliament, audited entities and, ultimately, our citizens.

It can be seen that challenges exist today for SAIs but that also the future presents unique challenges. These relate to demographic changes and demands by stakeholders from public services, and the need for assurance about the quality of these services. Technology may ease the pressures around the development of further tools or audit services, but there are expectations that better use will be made of data in order to comprehensively analyse public problems and highlight the risks that nations are facing. Resource constraints loom large on the agenda, requiring more of SAIs, especially as they are being enrolled in the push for sustainability, in particular in relation to monitoring and assurance of achievements of the Sustainable

Development Goals. Further, the realm of 'best practice' – the globalisation of audit forms and tools – is a current challenge. There is a need to homogenise and adapt good practices across different types of SAIs in different contexts. Nevertheless, in order to improve practice, it is also challenging to embed the learning from those different contexts.

We now turn to the implications of both the literature review and survey for the future.

4.4 Implications for the future

From the literature and survey, we observe evidence of a future that will differ from today in many respects. Table 4.1 summarises the issues.

Susskind and Susskind (2015) suggest that responses by professionals will show a bias in favour of the status quo. The anticipated changes noted by SAIs in their responses to our survey are also likely to show this bias. Nevertheless, the responses show that SAIs are anticipating and working on assurance services that better meet stakeholders' demands and have an eye to the future. SAIs are constrained by their legal mandate and the slowness with which public policy changes but are also mindful of their role in enhancing public sector efficiency and effectiveness.

In Chapter 3, the impact of isomorphism was canvassed. Coercive isomorphism factors were examined to explain why SAIs would use a particular model or move to the Westminster model. These were amount of aid, GDP and debt and stock market capitalisation. While coercive factors did not explain the SAI model, a question for the future is whether dramatic changes in debt levels (compared to GDP), or relative stock market capitalisation brought about by more countries in 'middle-income levels' (World Bank Group, 2015), will lead to changes in the dominance of the Westminster model. This is similar to mimetic isomorphism where the factors examined were a political stability index measure, the Freedom House rankings of political rights and civil liberties, the rule of law in a country and its colonial past (if any). These mimetic factors do appear to show the Westminster model as paramount, although the impact of forecasted political instability (National Intelligence Council, 2012) should be factored in. Lastly, normative factors were also examined: measures of education, the Brown *et al.* (2014) accounting standards measures and the use of International Financial Reporting Standards. The evidence suggests normative isomorphism is occurring with SAIs in countries with a strong auditing profession being more likely to apply the Westminster system. Again, these measures are subject to change. Further, more granular analysis may observe that future trends impact the types of audits undertaken and the range of entities audited (and by whom).

Table 4.1 Anticipated changes to public sector audit

Impact of change	*Anticipated change (from literature)*	*Compared to survey/practice*
Technology	• Greater use of technology (e.g. data analytics) to speed audit, monitoring and risk assessments. • Higher demands (and the ability to have) more transparency leads to 'armchair auditors' and the need for SAIs to link to them and yet maintain independence. • Cyber security risks will be higher, and IT audits will be in greater demand.	• 'Armchair auditors' not yet evident to any great extent. • Audit procedures for crypto-currencies and blockchain still in development.
Demography	• Changing demographics and increased demands for personalised services and audits thereof requires co-production (and will also stretch SAI resources). • Greater regulation from international investment requires careful audit.	• Potential changes in workforce not yet discussed. • New ways of working (and therefore new internal controls) not considered. • Joint audit not of concern.
Scarce resources	• Greater resource constraints drive demands for value for money and performance audits. • Requirements to audit national compliance with SDGs demands new skills in non-financial audit but also a strong SAI. Joint audits also required. • SAIs will be expected to carefully audit public debt and fiscal constraints – may have to critique government policies.	• Greater up-skilling and new ways to undertake these audits need to be worked on. • SDGs are an emerging audit area, and it is not clear how they will link to private sector contributions to SDGs. • Fiscal controls not yet discussed publicly.
Globalisation	• Best practice being sought in respect of standards and whole of government audit. • Unstable political environment brings unanticipated challenges that require new solutions. • Stakeholders have greater demands of SAIs and need for better communication (also tied to technology).	• Arguably less developed countries will learn from developed countries, but instability brings poor infrastructure and may require new methods to be developed. • New methods of performance audit not indicated.

The more likely changes in the future are the reasons why audit is demanded, or the value of audit. Chapter 2 introduced six different reasons for stakeholders to demand audit, and Chapter 3 examined two of them: agency theory and signalling. The most common form of SAI (the Westminster model) carried out the lowest average number of audits. Nevertheless, when asked for the reasons why stakeholders might demand audit, our SAI respondents suggested agency theory only one-third of the time, followed by management control and corporate governance (both at 21%), signalling (13%), insurance (7%) and confirmation (5%). The literature and the results of our survey suggest stronger demands from stakeholders in relation to accountability (encompassing potentially agency theory, management control and corporate governance). Will Westminster SAIs of the future have the capacity to respond to these demands? Further, with forecasted future resource scarcity and arguably higher debt levels, it is also likely that the demands for audit related to signalling will increase.

This chapter shows that the future, although uncertain, is likely to draw on the trends indicated by our review of the literature and our survey. While SAIs may not be able to anticipate different reasons for the demand for audit to change, they appear certain that stakeholders will demand more audit, that the timeframes for these audits will also reduce from where they are today and that the scope of SAI audits will increase. Due to the dominant type of SAI, there will be a need to scale-up to prepare for these greater demands. There will be unexpected changes, too. Perhaps the demands for change in the structure of private sector audits will have an impact on the public sector; or new reform movements may arise. Certainly, as governments change to respond to the pressures of the future, SAIs should also prepare for this uncertain future.

Notes

1 These reviews were the Statutory Audit Services study by the Competitions and Markets authority (December 2018) (see www.gov.uk/cma-cases/statutory-audit-market-study); the Independent Review of the Financial Reporting Council by Sir John Kingman (December 2018) (see www.gov.uk/government/publications/financial-reporting-council-review-2018); and The Independent Review into the Quality and Effectiveness of Audit by Sir Donald Brydon (Call for views April 2019) (see www.gov.uk/government/consultations/the-quality-and-effectiveness-of-audit-call-for-views).

2 This is now due to report back in September 2020. See: www.aph.gov.au/Parliamentary_Business/Committees/Joint/Corporations_and_Financial_Services/RegulationofAuditing

3 See: https://afm.nl/en/professionals/nieuws/2018/nov/kwetsbaarheden-structuur-accountancysector

4 See: www.cpacanada.ca/en/foresight-initiative

5 Exposure draft available at: www.intosaicbc.org/wp-content/uploads/2015/08/ISSAI-5800-final-draft_clean.pdf

References

Barrett, P. (1996) 'Some thoughts about the roles, responsibilities and future scope of Auditors-General', *Australian Journal of Public Administration*, 55(4), pp. 137–146.

Bititci, U. *et al.* (2012) 'Performance measurement: Challenges for tomorrow', *International Journal of Management Reviews*, 14(3), pp. 305–327. https://doi.org/10.1111/j.1468-2370.2011.00318.x.

Brown, P., Preiato, J. and Tarca, A. (2014) 'Measuring country differences in enforcement of accounting standards: An audit and enforcement proxy', *Journal of Business Finance and Accounting*, 41(1–2), pp. 1–52. https://doi.org/10.1111/jbfa.12066.

Carney, G. M. (2014) 'Commission on the voluntary sector & ageing: A policy review', *Voluntary Sector Review*, 5(2), pp. 203–211.

Chartered Institute of Public Finance and Accountancy and Public Finance (2005) *Protecting the Public Purse*. Available at: http://0-search.ebscohost.com.wam.city.ac.uk/login.aspx?direct=true&db=bth&AN=17111850&site=ehost-live.

Cordery, C. J. and Hay, D. (2018) 'Supreme Audit Institutions and public value: Demonstrating relevance', *Financial Accountability & Management*, 35(2), pp. 128–142.

Cuhls, K. (2003) 'From forecasting to foresight processes: New participative foresight activities in Germany', *Journal of Forecasting*, 22(2–3), pp. 93–111. https://doi.org/10.1002/for.848.

DiMaggio, P. J. and Powell, W. W. (1983) 'The iron cage revisited: Institutional isomorphism and collective rationality in organizational fields', *American Sociological Review*, 48(2), pp. 147–160.

European Commission (2012) *Global Europe 2050*. Directorate-General for Research and Innovation Socio-economic Science and Humanities European Commission, Luxembourg.

Federation of European Accountants (2014) *The Future of Audit and Assurance*. Federation of European Accountants, Brussels, Belgium. https://doi.org/10.1590/S1807-17752014000100002.

Ferry, L. and Eckersley, P. (2015) 'Budgeting and governing for deficit reduction in the UK public sector: Act three "accountability and audit arrangements"', *Public Money & Management*, 35(3), pp. 203–210. https://doi.org/10.1080/09540962.2015.1027496.

Forbes Insights and KPMG (2017) *Audit 2025: The Future is Now*. Forbes Insights, Jersey City, NJ, USA Grace, C. *et al.* (2012) *The Future of Public Audit*. Edited by C. Grace. London, UK: Solace Foundation.

Grasso, P. G. and Sharkansky, I. (2001) 'The auditing of public policy and the politics of auditing: The U.S. GAO and Israel's State Comptroller', *Governance*, 14(1), pp. 1–21. https://doi.org/10.1111/0952-1895.00149.

Hay, D. (2020) *The Future of Auditing*. Abingdon, Oxon, UK: Routledge.

IMF Fiscal Affairs (2020a) "Tax Issues: An Overview" Special Series on Fiscal Policies to Respond to Covid-19, Fiscal Affairs Department IMF, Washington DC, USA.
IMF Fiscal Affairs (2020b) "Public Sector Support to Firms" Special Series on Fiscal Policies to Respond to Covid-19, Fiscal Affairs Department IMF, Washington DC, USA.
Johnsen, Å. *et al.* (2019) 'Supreme audit institutions in a high-impact context: A comparative analysis of performance audit in four Nordic countries', *Financial Accountability & Management*, (December 2018), pp. 1–24. https://doi.org/10.1111/faam.12188.
KPMG Board Leadership Centre (2018) *The Future of Audit: A Note from KPMG's Audit Committee Institute*. KPMG International Cooperative, Geneva, Switzerland.
Monroe-Ellis, P. (2018) 'We have to be a beacon: Jamaica's AG reflects on SAI 's SDG journey', *International Journal of Government Auditing*, Autumn.
Mowat Centre (2014) *Future State 2030: The Global Megatrends Shaping Governments*. KPMG International Cooperative, Geneva, Switzerland.
National Intelligence Council (2012) *Global Trends 2030: Alternative Worlds*. National Intelligence Council. Virginia, USA. ISBN 978-1-929667-21-5.
Normanton, E. L. (1966) *The Accountability and Audit of Governments*. Manchester: Manchester University Press.
O'Leary, D. E. (2015) 'Armchair auditors: Crowdsourcing analysis of government expenditures', *Journal of Emerging Technologies in Accounting*, 12(1), pp. 71–91. https://doi.org/10.2308/jeta-51225.
Power, Michael K. 2003. "Auditing and the Production of Legitimacy." *Accounting, Organizations and Society* 28(4): 379–94.
Pöysti, T. (2007) 'Future of Public Audit and Accountability', in *European Court of Auditors' Seminar on "The future of public auditing and accountability in the European Union"*, National Audit Office, Luxembourg. p. 7.
PricewaterhouseCoopers (2014) *The Future of Work – A Journey to 2022*. PricewaterhouseCoopers New Zealand, Wellington, NZ. https://doi.org/10.1108/ws.1999.07948gaf.002.
PricewaterhouseCoopers (2019) *The Future of Audit*. PricewaterhouseCoopers LLP, London, UK. https://doi.org/10.2469/cfm.v27.n3.18.
Rajaguguk, B. W., Yatnaputra, I. G. B. T. and Paulus, A. (2017) 'Preparing supreme audit insitutions for susainable development goals', *International Journal of Government Auditing*, Spring.
Reichborn-Kjennerud, K. *et al.* (2019) 'SAIs work against corruption in Scandinavian, South-European and African countries: An institutional analysis', *British Accounting Review*, 51(5). https://doi.org/10.1016/j.bar.2019.100842.
Ryan, B. (2012) 'Co-production: Option or obligation?', *Australian Journal of Public Administration*, 71(3), pp. 314–324. https://doi.org/10.1111/j.1467-8500.2012.00780.x.
Salijeni, G., Samsonova-Taddei, A. and Turley, S. (2019) 'Big Data and changes in audit technology: Contemplating a research agenda', *Accounting and Business Research*. Taylor & Francis, 49(1), pp. 95–119. https://doi.org/10.1080/00014788.2018.1459458.

Schwartz, J. *et al.* (2019) 'What is the future of work? Redefining work, workforces, and workplaces', *Deloitte Insights*, (April), pp. 1–12. http://doi.org/10.1001/archsurg.138.8.825.

Siddiqui, J. (2019) *Are Four Eyes Better than Two? An Examination of Recent Empirical Evidence on the Impact of Joint Audits*. University of Manchester, Manchester, UK.

Simon, B. (2019) *The Future of Audit*. Available at: The future of audit My Account Store Contact Français%0AThe CPA Profession%0ABecome a CPA%0AEarn the ACAF%0ACareer and Professional Development%0ABusiness and%0AAccounting Resources%0ATHE CANADIAN IDEAL OF GOOD BUSINESS.%0AMembers' Area%0ANews Home/News (Accessed: 20 August 2019).

Susskind, R. and Susskind, D. (2015) *The Future of the Professions: How Technology Will Transform the Work of Human Experts*. ebook. Oxford: Oxford University Press.

van Helden, J. and Uddin, S. (2016) 'Public sector management accounting in emerging economies: A literature review', *Critical Perspectives on Accounting*. Elsevier Ltd, 41, pp. 34–62. https://doi.org/10.1016/j.cpa.2016.01.001.

World Bank Group (2015) *Purchasing Power Parities and the Real Size of World Economies*. Washington, DC: World Bank.

Yamamoto, K. and Kim, M. J. (2019) 'Stakeholders' approach on government auditing in the supreme audit institutions of Japan and Korea', *Financial Accountability & Management*, (June 2018), pp. 1–16. https://doi.org/10.1111/faam.12187.

Yeoman, I. (2012) *2050 – Tomorrow's Tourism*. Channel View Publications. Bristol, United Kingdom.

5 Overview of main themes and projections

5.1 Introduction

This book considers the current context and types of public sector entity and future challenges for public sector audit. It is evident from the research we have analysed that the structures within which public sector audit is practised vary across the world; indeed, when SAIs are invited to self-identify to a model or models, the structures are much more diverse than prior literature suggests. While in Chapter 2 the objectives of public audit were canvassed, Chapter 3 provides details on these structures and the roles of numerous variables in driving the choice of structures. Chapter 4 analysed current and future issues identified both from literature and from the results of the survey that was commissioned for this book. In this chapter, we provide an overview of the main themes and ask whether and how the challenges and opportunities in the prior chapters could lead to developing new ways of audit in the public sector that could be useful to the private sector, or that could result in the public sector borrowing or adapting from the private sector. In addition to a reflection on these themes, we also note opportunities for future research and study.

5.2 Main themes

5.2.1 Structural variety mixed with isomorphism

Drawing on extant literature, in Chapter 1 we presented three SAI models (Westminster, board and court). Nevertheless, the empirical research we undertook and reported in Chapters 2 and 3 show that in reality these models are at best generalisations. Yet, research into SAIs seldom discusses this variety, often assuming homogeneity with a very few placing their research into the three- (World Bank) or four-model system. It appears that the desire to generalise can exclude SAIs that do not fit neatly into a particular model.

Notwithstanding the isomorphism towards particular models (specifically the Westminster model is widely cited), the operation of an SAI will reflect contextual differences. SAI independence from government is believed to underpin audit quality (Clark *et al*., 2007), yet a comparative case study of the Board of Audit of Japan and the Board of Audit and Inspection of Korea (Yamamoto and Kim, 2019) shows that the understanding of independence can differ, even when countries operate the same model. The difference between these two countries in terms of independence surrounds the issue of who can demand that the SAI should undertake an audit. Yamamoto and Kim (2019) explain that the Board of Audit of Japan fiercely resists stakeholder intervention and has full discretion on acceding to audit requests, whereas the Board of Audit and Inspection of Korea perceives citizens as direct stakeholders and must respond to request for audits if more than 300 citizens (or Civil Society Organisations with more than 300 members) request one, and must complete audits requested by the National Assembly within three months. Both SAIs seek to balance independence with meeting stakeholders' needs, but the understanding of independence differs. Many other examples of differences relating to context and historical factors could be provided in terms of structure.

As the analysis in this book has been cross-sectional, not longitudinal, due to data availability, we have not traced trends towards particular types of audit and emphases; nevertheless, we have provided an overview on which others can build. We noted (in Chapter 3) that a small number of SAIs report that they carry out financial and performance auditing only (see Table 3.6 and associated discussion), whereas compliance audits remain strong in some countries that may have been later in reforming their public management systems (see, for example, Kontogeorga, 2019). Kontogeorga (2019) notes that for a number of decades the IMF has been extolling performance audits to provide better information about effectiveness and efficiency of the public sector. INTOSAI also encourages performance audits as part of the suite of audits that SAIs undertake. It would be useful to compare and contrast the data used in this book with that from a different time period to ascertain how isomorphism is affecting the types of audits that are undertaken, for example the shift of resources towards performance audits and away from compliance audits. A further factor that could affect the audit mix (in addition to public management reform) will be the technological development of accounting and auditing information systems, which could take the place of human compliance audits in the public sector.

While we have focused only on nation states and their Supreme Audit Institutions undertaking external audits, we note that public sector audit extends beyond merely national concerns, not only in terms of state auditors in a federation but also to international organisations, such as the OECD and the UN. Indeed, Monfardini and von Maravic (2019) outline growing isomorphism in the arrangements for auditing these supra-national organisations. These auditing arrangements are worthy of further research. Further, INTOSAI's Development Initiative works with developing countries' SAIs[1] to develop capacity, and this process will be isomorphic on the countries with which they work.

5.2.2 Demands for audit are under-stated

The main reason for audit is due to principal-agent relationships, of which there are multiple levels in the public sector, and the ensuing need to ameliorate the issues related to information asymmetry. One aspect of information asymmetry is that it allows for an agent to defraud the principal. Reichborn-Kjennerud *et al.* (2019) report on the new ISSAI standard (ISSAI 5700) Guideline for the Audit of Corruption Prevention released in 2016 and how seven different nations have responded to the encouragement to fight corruption. The two African countries in their study (Uganda and Zambia) were working strongly on combatting corruption, as was Sweden, while they reported that Norway and Spain were responding at a "medium" level and Denmark and Italy only "weakly". This shows that the potential for public sector audit to contribute to the economy (in terms of reduced corruption) is under-stated and provides a continuing reason for agency theory to underpin the demand for public sector audit. In Chapter 4 we suggested that fraud may increase as governments increasingly fund private sector initiatives; therefore, the identification and reduction in fraud and corruption may increasingly fall to SAIs as they seek to increase citizens' trust in government.

In Chapter 3 we show a number of other variables that confirm the usefulness of agency theory principles in public sector audit. We also examined debt as a variable that would underpin a signalling explanation for audit. While Lamoreaux *et al.* (2015) argued that development loans were higher for countries with higher accounting quality and a stronger audit environment, our analysis does not show this signalling effect. The lack of a full dataset has impaired this analysis.

Nevertheless, the responses from our survey show that the SAI respondents believed that the management control and corporate governance explanations were second equally after agency theory in explaining why audit is demanded. Apart from Hay and Cordery (2020), there is a paucity of analysis of these other demands for audit.

In Chapter 4, we reported that SAIs believe that stakeholders' demands will change in the future, requiring more transparency, more focus on reform, more effectiveness and more efficiency. This will require SAIs to develop new ways of communicating with stakeholders to meet their needs, as well as changes in legislation in order to empower SAIs to do so. We note further that the private sector survey by Forbes Insights and KPMG (2017, p. 2) found that auditors "need to be more forward-looking". If auditors respond to these demands, it will signal a change in practice. In addition, it is likely to increase the demand for new audit standards to enable SAIs to meet these needs. These changing stakeholder demands suggest the existence of a public sector audit-expectation gap. Despite the wide discussion of the expectation gap in the private sector (Porter, 2014), this was a surprising lack from both the literature review and survey undertaken for this book. Despite the audit-expectation gap being a focus of a number of the recent government and professions' enquiries into private sector audit, it is a relatively unexplored area in the public sector that is worthy of further research.

While we recognise that individual nations differ, we note that there is a number of issues discussed in the private sector that have lower visibility in the public sector. For example, audit rotation, an issue discussed in various private sector reviews (e.g. the Brydon review and CPA Canada Foresight), is not highlighted for public sector audit as to ensure audit quality SAIs seek independence. Linked to this is the development of joint audits, seldom undertaken in the private sector but very much a part of public sector audit, as shown by Monfardini and von Maravic (2019). Public sector expertise in joint (or combined) audits is one area where the public sector could assist private sector auditors in understanding the benefits and drawbacks of cooperative audits.

Another aspect of private sector audit that has been implicated in improving the quality of audits is improved corporate governance (for example, Forbes Insights and KPMG, 2017; PricewaterhouseCoopers, 2019). This has received far less attention in research about public sector audit, which seldom considers internal audit and the role of corporate governance in improving audit quality and reducing risk. Further, given demands for greater transparency in audit as shown in Chapter 4 and by Forbes Insights and KPMG (2017), demands for reporting on Key Audit Matters and other risk-based assessments are likely to increase. Expanded use of Key Audit Matters will also assist public sector audit quality (International Organization of Supreme Audit Institutions, 2016).

5.2.3 Public sector audit is valued

It is apparent that public sector audit is of value to stakeholders and that demands will continue to grow. Strong SAIs deliver value in independent, high-quality audits that can also be used to improve practices (Cordery and Hay, 2018). The mix of audits undertaken that deliver this value are as diverse as SAI structures.

Performance audits, which have developed since the New Public Management reforms, have been shown to assist in holding an agent to account, in some countries, but also to improve practice in public sector organisations, making them learning opportunities and likely to reflect the demand for audit from a corporate governance point of view (Johnsen *et al.*, 2019). The different uses of a performance audit and the context in which they are undertaken may also impact the requirement for independence. Tillema and ter Bogt (2016) studied performance audits in local government and found that, while audit demands motivated by agency theory are concerned with formal independence, when performance audits are undertaken in an atmosphere of collaboration and trust as with stewardship theory, operational independence is valued more. Such performance audits are more likely to create learning opportunities and will be valued as such, suggesting that independence needs different foci when stakeholders seek added value.

SAIs' experiences with performance audits and the audit of non-financial data represent an expertise from which private sector auditors could learn. Increasingly, investors and analysts are relying on non-financial information and non-GAAP measures, and the audit of these is problematic, both technically and in encouraging corporates to develop measures that are robust.[2] Indeed, the rise of products such as integrated reporting suggests fields where public and private sector auditors can jointly develop further expertise.

5.3 Conclusion

As we enter the beginning of the third decade of the 21st century, the need for public sector audit remains as strong as it has ever been. Political instability, bringing lower levels of citizen trust and scarcity of economic and environmental resources, all signal the need for greater accountability and transparency. Public sector audit can assist governments to deliver this and assist the public sector to achieve greater levels of efficiency and effectiveness.

The continued move of countries to accrual accounting (especially public sector financial reporting standards) and the development of auditing standards and support from INTOSAI and its regional SAI bodies point to the likelihood of a higher quality audit. Therefore, despite a crisis in private sector audit, Supreme Audit Institutions have opportunities to continue to add value and to learn.

Notes

1 See: www.idi.no/en/
2 CPA Foresight. See: www.cpacanada.ca/en/foresight-initiative (see also PricewaterhouseCoopers, 2019).

References

Clark, C. *et al.* (2007) 'Audit quality attributes of European Union supreme audit institutions', *European Business Review*, 19, pp. 40–71. https://doi.org/10.1108/09555340710714144.

Cordery, C. J. and Hay, D. (2018) 'Supreme audit institutions and public value: Demonstrating relevance', *Financial Accountability & Management*, 35(2), pp. 128–142.

Forbes Insights and KPMG (2017) *Audit 2025: The Future is Now*. Forbes Insights, New York, NY.

Hay, D. and Cordery, C. J. (2020) 'Evidence about the value of financial statement audit in the public sector', *Public Money & Management*. Taylor & Francis, pp. 1–11. https://doi.org/10.1080/09540962.2020.1729532.

International Organization of Supreme Audit Institutions (2016) *Competency Framework for Public Sector Audit Professionals at Supreme Audit Institutions*. International Organization of Supreme Audit Institutions, Vienna, Austria.

Johnsen, Å. *et al.* (2019) 'Supreme audit institutions in a high-impact context: A comparative analysis of performance audit in four Nordic countries', *Financial Accountability & Management*, (December 2018), pp. 1–24. https://doi.org/10.1111/faam.12188.

Kontogeorga, G. N. (2019) 'Juggling between ex-ante and ex-post audit in Greece: A difficult transition to a new era', *International Journal of Auditing*, 23(1), pp. 86–94. https://doi.org/10.1111/ijau.12147.

Lamoreaux, P. T. *et al.* (2015) 'Do accounting and audit quality affect World Bank lending?', *The Accounting Review*, 90(2), pp. 703–738.

Monfardini, P. and von Maravic, P. (2019) 'Too big to be audited? The new world of auditing in international organizations', *Financial Accountability and Management*, 35(2), pp. 143–157. https://doi.org/10.1111/faam.12186.

Porter, B. A. (2014) 'The audit expectation gap', in Hay, D., Knechel, W. R., and Willekens, M. (eds.), *The Routledge Companion to Auditing*. Abingdon, Oxon, UK: Routledge.

PricewaterhouseCoopers (2019) *The Future of Audit*. PricewaterhouseCoopers LLP, London, UK. https://doi.org/10.2469/cfm.v27.n3.18.

Reichborn-Kjennerud, K. *et al.* (2019) 'SAIs work against corruption in Scandinavian, South-European and African countries: An institutional analysis', *British Accounting Review*, 51(5). https://doi.org/10.1016/j.bar.2019.100842.

Tillema, S. and ter Bogt, H. J. (2016) 'Does an agency-type of audit model fit a stewardship context? Evidence from performance auditing in Dutch municipalities', *Financial Accountability and Management*, 32(2), pp. 135–156. https://doi.org/10.1111/faam.12084.

Yamamoto, K. and Kim, M. J. (2019) 'Stakeholders' approach on government auditing in the supreme audit institutions of Japan and Korea', *Financial Accountability & Management*, (June 2018), pp. 1–16. https://doi.org/10.1111/faam.12187.

Index

Note: Page locators in **bold** indicate a table and page locators in *italic* indicate a figure on the corresponding page.

www.ingramcontent.com/pod-product-compliance
Ingram Content Group UK Ltd.
Pitfield, Milton Keynes, MK11 3LW, UK
UKHW021512250926
475702UK00043B/80
* 9 7 8 0 3 6 7 1 9 2 9 1 4 *